MISGUIDED LIBERALS

MISGUIDED LIBERALS

39 DUMB REASONS THE LEFT DOESN'T VOTE RIGHT

WYATT ELLIS

CONTENTS

INTRODUCTION

The Premise

The working title of this book was *Not All Liberals Are Stupid.* Sometimes when we disagree with people, we resort to name-calling. And I had wrongly come to the conclusion over a number of years that Americans who continually identified as liberal, progressive, or generally supported the Democratic party and its causes were stupid. How could they not see how the ideas of the left were based on ridiculous notions and led to bad results? But then I started to think about my own experience with liberals. They weren't just talking heads on TV. They were colleagues, friends, and even family. Surely, I couldn't dismiss them all as stupid. So I started to think of what drove millions of people, many of whom I knew to be quite intelligent, to side with a political movement that my own research and logic had found to be so errant. I came up with a list of reasons based on specific people I knew and segments of society I had learned about. I realized that there were many reasons, wrong as they were, that liberals were liberals.

I soon realized maybe the title I had in place didn't necessarily convey the premise I had intended. But the original idea still is the core of this book. *Not all* liberals are stupid. In case you were under the wrong impression, no, this book is not designed to defend liberals from unjust accusations. In fact, the working title may have certainly been an insult toward those on the left, but it was really more of a reminder to myself and those like me who get frustrated with liberals, to not resort to angry eruptions like, "They're so stupid!"

Many are. But just as liberals are wrong when they claim conservatives are "idiots," so too are conservatives speaking incorrectly when they talk about their counterparts on the left. The brutal truth, as much as it pains us to admit it, is a lot of progressives are actually not dumb. Can we really deny that Bill Clinton is intelligent? As much damage as he did to this country, it's not because he's a fool. In fact, I don't believe George W. Bush is a fool, even though he's been portrayed that way constantly. He certainly is not a great speaker, and frankly, I didn't agree with many of his policies. But still, I think we're wrong to call him an idiot.

Barack Obama isn't an idiot. It would be great if he were, because then we could blame his disastrous approach to government on his intellectual shortcomings. But he is smart. As much as it pains me to say it, it's true.

So then what is it? Why are liberals… liberals? How can they say things that drive us up the wall? How can they be so against everything that common sense, experience, economics, and more importantly, the Constitution, stand for?

This book seeks to explore the answer to that question. It is not meant to persuade anyone that my political beliefs are correct. It is not a guide to facts, history, statistics, and all those things that *I* personally have turned to which have made me who I am politically. In fact, you'll notice that while there are references in the back of the book, I don't usually get into specifics to prove why, for instance, a policy of the left has failed. Why? As good as I think I am at identifying the reasons people on the left are on the left, I don't think I can do nearly as good a job at marshalling the data and the well-developed arguments on the issues as my sources have. What you will find, however, is a list of sources by chapter, as well as a recommended reading section, which lists authors and organizations whose work clearly illustrates the conservative/libertarian viewpoint and whose writings have informed my beliefs tremendously. These writers and researchers do a far better job than I ever could, and I encourage any liberal, moderate, or even full-fledged conservative to read as many of these selections as possible.

No, this book is simply designed to explore what has brought so many millions of people to keep identifying as liberal. I will discuss in general why they're bad reasons, but that's not really the point of the book.

How would I *prove* why liberals are liberal anyway? Even if they make statements about their beliefs, that doesn't give proof as to what they really believe, or why they vote for certain people. I am therefore relying on my experiences and intuition to reach my conclusions. You don't have to believe me, but I think you will. I am hopeful that you will recognize some of the liberals in your own life, in public life, or even yourself, as not stupid, but certainly a liberal, always for very bad reasons.

Where does this insight come from? I am not your typical conservative. I'm much more a libertarian. I don't capitalize it because I'm not a member of the Libertarian Party. What is a libertarian? Basically, a libertarian or "classical liberal" is a person who recognizes that the government, especially the federal government, was given extremely limited powers in the Constitution. They are to protect our lives and property from enemies foreign and domestic. (No, that doesn't mean providing health care at the expense of everyone else.) A libertarian believes that people should be free to lead their lives as they choose, so long as they are not interfering with the lives of others. So in this book, you may see a few areas where I agree with liberals, almost always in terms of social issues. I apologize if this offends some of my more Republican-minded fellow conservatives, but I think you will still be able to find entertainment and insight within these pages. "Socially liberal," though, doesn't really define me either, as I'm not a fan of safe spaces, self-imposed victimhood, the Black Lives Matter organization or movement, or being required to refer to individuals with pronouns like "they" rather than he or she. And even when I do find some agreement with progressives, I still recognize that those positions aren't good enough reasons to justify considering oneself a liberal, or worse, supporting a whole slew of policies that are so destructive.

Furthermore, this book does not excuse people who vote for Republicans for "dumb" reasons either. There are plenty of them, undoubtedly. Likewise, there are plenty of books, movies, TV shows, celebrities, and so on who tear into Republicans on a daily basis, often viciously and with hypocrisy. There's no need to pile onto that. That's just not what this particular book is about.

In fact, I have never voted for a Republican presidential candidate. I certainly didn't vote for their Democratic challengers either. I chose a third party candidate, not because I was deluded into thinking he or she would win, but because I refused to vote for someone who would only grow the size of government.

What makes my experience somewhat unique is a combination of factors. While my parents were middle class and I grew up in the San Fernando Valley in Los Angeles, I was brought up in a wealthy, liberal Jewish community via my education at a private Jewish day school in nearby Bel Air. Presumably in need of a massive culture shock, I then went to a large public high school in Van Nuys, in the Los Angeles Unified School District. In my P.E. class, I was the only "white" kid in a class of about 40. I went on to receive a Bachelor of Arts in Political Science at UCLA, worked a couple years in the entertainment industry, and am now a teacher at a public elementary school. I also write musicals on the side.

The odds would be against me turning out to be a conservative/libertarian. Let me repeat. I live in Los Angeles. I'm Jewish. I worked in the entertainment industry and am now a teacher. I went to UCLA. I studied Political Science at UCLA. Did I mention I write musicals? These are not the typical characteristics of a conservative, even a libertarian one.

While my family was never extremely political, I soon grew frustrated with the state of things around me. My taxpayer-funded public school had gangs, although I was fortunately never a direct victim. Most of the students at my school would never graduate, and crimes would often be committed in the area surrounding the school, as well as within. My frustration with the abundance of criminal activity grew when my bicycle was stolen outside my high school, and soon after when my car was broken into and the stereo was taken. As it became time to apply to college, I discovered just how much tougher the requirements would be for me than my fellow students who happened to have a different skin color, due to Affirmative Action. Together, these experiences led me to conservative political philosophy in general, which seemed to go hand in hand with the Republican Party.

But soon I began listening to radio talk show host and future gubernatorial candidate Larry Elder, a "republitarian" as he called himself, who happens to be African-American. I read several of his books and listened as often as possible to his radio show. I was even fortunate enough to meet him a few times. His arguments were so effective, and the surprising facts that he seemed to have memorized were things that I had never heard before. I soon realized that personal re-sponsibility was one of the key ideas that resonated with me when it came to being against crime and against Affirmative Action. Learning from Elder that the government actually causes a lot more problems than it solves only shored up my beliefs in personal responsibility and helped me realize that the common factor in so many of society's problems was the overextended reach of government.

I soon read from other sources with a libertarian bent and the arguments made and the data provided as evidence always came off as so much more rational than the clichéd talking points I had heard all my life from people on the left. In college, I took a basic economics class by a visiting young professor. We learned about supply and demand, and the effects of artificial adjustments to the free market, such as minimum wage and rent control. Even at a bastion of liberalism such as UCLA, the facts just couldn't be hidden.

I began taking in the works of Thomas Sowell, Milton Friedman, F.A. Hayek, Thomas Jefferson, John Stossel, Andrew Napolitano, the folks at Reason Magazine and the Cato Institute, and many others. By the time I got to Ayn Rand, I needed no more convincing and was able to just enjoy *The Fountainhead* and *Atlas Shrugged*. Along the way, I realized, too, that I didn't agree with many Republicans either, as I found them to be too willing to use the force of government to impose their socially restrictive ideas, or hardly any better than the folks on the left when it came to government spending.

I've learned through this process (and in my career as a teacher) that most of societal problems are due to bad parenting. But when it comes to politics, it's an issue of government overstepping its bounds. I boil it down to the "Big Four," which I will refer to throughout this book. The Big Four is my own essential collection of the four big reasons why we should be saying no to nearly any given proposal, policy or law put into place by the federal government (and often state and local governments, too). They are often, but certainly not always, enacted at the hands of Democrats. **The Big Four reasons most of these ideas are wrong is because they ignore ethics, the Constitution, history, and economics.**

First, ethics. Most of the government's programs and actions are immoral, as they essentially take money by the force of a gun from one person to give to another. When you don't pay your taxes for someone else's pet cause, you get fined and have to now pay more of your own money. If it happens repeatedly, you could wind up behind bars. You shouldn't have to pay for charitable causes you don't agree with in the first place (welfare, Medicare, Medicaid, etc.), especially when so many of them are so horribly inefficient and prevent more effective alternatives from helping those in need.

Next, the Constitution. Government programs are almost always unconstitutional, as they go far beyond the limits of federal power espoused in the United States Constitution. The Constitution, despite being written a long time ago (see that chapter later), is the only restraint we have to prevent our government from making the same mistakes as all its predecessors.

Third, history. If we look at this country's past, we'd see that when government wasn't heavily involved, the free market and charitable societies provided for people in need far more effectively, efficiently, cheaply, and without the threat of violence than these leviathan programs do now. Roads and trains were built, people received medical care and education, and the poor got financial support. The doom-and-gloom scenarios associated with the government *not* doing everything it currently does now are just not aligned with reality or history.

And fourth, economics. These government actions have tons of implications economically. Part of that includes negative effects on the choices people make: less saving if your money's being taken for Social Security, less working and more single-parent homes if you get rewarded for such behavior in various welfare programs, and rising healthcare prices because of so many regulations on insurance companies, hospitals, and drug manufacturers. And we've seen what happens when a country's economy fails, when its government spends more than it can afford. The economy grinds to a halt, leading to mass unemployment, stock market crashes (along with our retirement savings), skyrocketing of prices on everything we need to survive, uptick in mortgage rates meaning fewer people able to own a home, and – ironically, as it is one of the biggest culprits in the first place – the welfare state stops making its payments to recipients. Let's not even think about the inevitable riots that will result, as they did in Greece, Venezuela, and elsewhere.

Before going further, let's address an issue in semantics. There are many figures out there who draw a clear distinction between terms like "liberals" and "the left." There is a whole PragerU video that differentiates between "left" and "liberal," basically saying that the "left" is actually anti-liberal on race, capitalism, nationalism, their view of America, free speech, and Western civilization. I don't disagree with this at all. However, to avoid repeating the same words constantly, I may interchange "left," "liberal," and "progressive" throughout the book. For our purposes here, those terms basically just mean people who vote for Democrats and support their policies.

Needless to say, I'm in a somewhat unique situation, but certainly there are others out there like me. I have been surrounded by liberals my whole life, from all walks of life. On many occasions, I've made the mistake of engaging in debate with them, not realizing that it would always lead to their eruptions of anger and personal attacks no matter how calm and rational I stayed. And through these interactions, as well as through gleaning all I could from the statements and actions of public personalities, I've learned their reasons for being liberals. No, they're not all stupid. But they're all wrong.

They Are Slaves to Emotion

*"If this goes through, kiss life on earth goodbye.
The debate on health care is like death. This
is Armageddon." — Nancy Pelosi (D-CA), United
States House of Representatives, speaking about
a tax bill that ended the Obamacare mandate*

Many liberal causes and political positions are the obvious choices for people who let their feelings override logic and facts. Whether it's the supporters of the welfare state or lovers of single payer health care, people who are guided solely by what tugs at their heartstrings at a given moment are more likely to veer left. Why? Is it because liberals are kind and conservatives aren't? Of course not. Conservatives, in fact, tend to give much more to charity actually. It's because conservative — and to a greater degree, libertarian viewpoints – require some careful thought, moving beyond mere gut reactions. Once one pushes past the initial heart tremors, one can look at things like data, economics, and unintended consequences.

Don't get me wrong. Plenty of conservatives and libertarians are emotional, too, but Americans who never get beyond emotions, who never seek out facts from other sources, or who refuse to use reason and logic, tend to be on the left.

They hear about a school shooting, for instance. Like any decent human being, they are saddened by the vulnerability of our children and the tragic loss. But rather than do deep research using a variety of sources, they immediately say we need more "common-sense" gun control. They don't stop to ask questions: What gun control do we already have? What specific measures would you propose? Can they be realistically implemented? Even if they could, would they make any difference? Would those new laws hurt millions of people who just want to defend themselves and their families, including those who live in areas of poverty and crime, such as the inner city? How many women who carry a gun to defend themselves against stronger male attackers would be affected?

But emotion pervades liberal thought on a myriad of issues. When they think about destitute senior citizens, the poor, the homeless, or whatever group seems in need of their sympathy, liberals don't often look at the reality. They don't ask whether the elderly are as impoverished as they think, whether the "poor" in our country are really in need of more government assistance, or whether those programs actually do more harm than good in terms of dependence, such as incentivizing single moms to have more children for whom they can't provide.

Again, their gut reactions prevent them from asking, where is the money going to come from? Is it fair to take more and more from people without their explicit permission? Will it do any good? What will be the negative effects of confiscating money from one sector of the economy for some perceived injustice? Has this particular policy actually ever worked in the past? Is it constitutional? Moral?

No, those enslaved by emotion just see a cause that tugs at their heartstrings. They fail to go any further than sharing a *Washington Post* or *New York Times* article that says how uncaring Republicans are on that particular subject.

If liberals would only pause, take a breath, and ask some of these hard questions, look at other points of view (and no, that doesn't necessarily mean Fox News or Breitbart.com), maybe they could make political decisions based on logic and not "the feels."

They Are Uninformed

"If we work our butts off to make sure that we take back all three chambers of Congress — uh, rather, all three chambers of government: the presidency, the Senate, and the House..." — Alexandria Ocasio-Cortez (D-NY), United States House of Representatives, wrongly identifying the three branches of the federal government

It's a wonder that only about half of voters picked Hillary Clinton in the 2016 presidential election, and that Republican candidates still manage to win roughly as many elections as Democrats nationwide, with Senate and House party majorities going on a roughly cyclical pattern. I won't even get into the controversial 2020 election between Joseph Biden and Donald Trump, which was also "nearly" even at 51% and 46% according to stated tallies.

The point is that you would think that given the incredibly biased media and educational system, both of which indoctrinate so much of our population simply due to mass access, this would result in nearly 100 percent of our citizens voting for Democrats. And yet still, the bias inherent in our biggest social institutions – the media and schools, from kindergarten through graduate school – has clearly impacted a huge segment of the population. Those entities, while purporting to give citizens accurate and unbiased information, are together another big reason why liberals are who they are. It's simple – many liberals have just never heard any point of view other than their own, thoughtfully explained to them, or if they have heard an opposing opinion, it was filtered through the prism of fellow liberals and the perspective of those who held it wasn't provided. Or maybe that opinion was given via an extremist caricature from the right, like an Alex Jones, that the left wing media was purposely showcasing.

Fox News is of course the go-to target for liberals who complain about conservative bias. The truth is that besides their opinion shows featuring conservative figures like Sean Hannity, Tucker Carlson, and Greg Gutfeld, the actual news coverage, while admittedly slanted to the right, is not the Republican Party mouthpiece its leftist critics bash it as. If you watch a *news* program on Fox News, not only do both sides of the aisle get picked apart, but panels of guest commentators are usually a decent mix of political opinions, too. But if you're used to watching shows on the vast majority of network and cable television news or reading articles from most major newspapers or online sites like The Huffington Post, then your impression of Fox News is going to be skewed. Fox News, one of few media outlets (and certainly the biggest) which actually covers stories that make Democrats look bad, not just Republicans, certainly could seem like an alien, far-right extremist organization. If you're used to drinking water your whole life, and suddenly have orange juice, it may likely seem like hydrochloric acid.

There is a lot that liberals may not know about Fox News though. They may not know, for instance, that former president Donald Trump has had plenty of criticism for the network. They may not know that several figures on the news side have said Trump's stolen election allegations were not backed up by evidence. They may also not know that the network alienated many conservatives when it ran a positive story about a "trans-identified" child during "Pride Month." They may not know that the longtime host of *Fox News Sunday* was a registered Democrat who criticized Trump's treatment of the press. Ironically, all liberals know is what they're fed from their own extremely biased sources about how evil and extreme Fox News is.

If you do spend any time watching one of the other major news outlets, not even counting the extremes like MSNBC, you can find constant reporting bias. Most people don't recognize it because it's all they've been used to for their entire lives. It's hard to believe they don't see the obvious bias in the aforementioned MSNBC, Salon, Huffington Post, CNN, the Nation, NPR, and the *New York Times*, but perhaps it's easier to understand how the strong bias of the seemingly "right-down-the-middle" *Newsweek*, *Time*, broadcast network nightly news, and Associated Press goes unnoticed. Those all seem like mainstream, moderate sources to liberals because they're all they've ever consumed.

How does the bias appear? It comes out in the selection of which stories to cover, and which ones to skip. It rears its head in the ranking of search engine results, and the wording of headlines and on-screen TV graphics. It shows its face in the types of questions asked to one candidate versus another, for instance. Liberals loved Katie Couric asking Sarah Palin what newspapers and magazines she read. Would Couric have ever dreamed of asking that of Nancy Pelosi? It's an insulting question in the first place, and just one of many instances of left-wing bias. And of course it comes in the form of supposedly unbiased journalists giving their viewpoints on the story from a distinctly liberal perspective.

In our education system, bias is also always there. History books give value to US presidents who engaged in government-enlarging actions in the name of helping society, instilling the notion in young minds that such actions are necessarily good. When dark-skinned peoples fought light-skinned peoples, the former are generally presented as the victims, when sometimes the reality was not so crystal clear. Diversity of race is always the promoted concept, whereas diversity of thought – not so much. The wealthy are presented as evil fat cats, with little to no attention on their rise from rags to riches or how society was immeasurably better because of them. Students are led to think, for instance, that unrestricted monopolies like Standard Oil and greedy capitalists like John D. Rockefeller proved the dangers of unregulated capitalism, when it turns out all of that was a lie. Educators instill other plainly wrong ideas, such as the notion that the Progressive Era was essential to our progress, when it turns out that its components were actually completely unnecessary and unbelievably destructive.

With the majority of Americans being brought up in a system where their lives are dominated by such a strong liberal bias, most liberals just don't know anything else. They've never considered that what they've been told their whole lives is wrong. They've never stopped to think, hold on, my college professor wants me to believe what she believes, or my eighth-grade textbook was written by people in the government education crowd who clearly want me to come to their way of thinking. Liberals have never stopped while watching (now disgraced anchor) Matt Lauer or Wolf Blitzer to say, wait a minute, this guy's got an agenda and wants me to buy the ideas he's selling.

Liberals are not just consumers of this bias; they are also its producers. Liberals flock to the field of education, populating most teacher positions and certainly predominating the ranks of most institutions of higher learning. Polls of news reporters have revealed time and time again that most vote Democratic. This is no big secret. Is it any wonder then, that after living in a society so dominated by such opinions that most Americans simply don't have the desire, the individuality, or yes, even the ability to escape it? Fox News and AM talk radio are certainly not the only other options for hearing non-leftist opinions, even though that's what liberals think. But believing they are the only choices makes alternative thought easy to dismiss.

If only liberals would take the time to step outside their shell and question everything they've been told, to realize there are other sources out there besides their teachers and the mainstream media, and that nearly everything that's presented to them in newspapers, TV, and the Internet has an inherent liberal bias, they might be able to establish newly informed beliefs and make better decisions about whom to vote for.

They Are Obsessed with LGBTQIA+ "Rights"

"It's normal... It's normalized. It's not anything strange. It's not strange. Remember, Anderson? Back 15, 20 years ago when we talked about this in San Francisco, it was all about, well, gay bath houses. It was all about round-the-clock sex. Come on, man. Gay couples are more likely to stay together longer than heterosexual couples." —President Joe Biden (before being elected) pandering at a Democratic Party presidential debate hosted by CNN's Anderson Cooper

f you talk long enough to anyone who calls themselves a liberal, Democrat, or progressive you'll quickly discover that many base their entire political alignment on just one relatively minor issue: LGBTQIA+ "rights." This is not to say that it's unreasonable for anyone to value the general idea of fairness and equal rights for all human beings. In fact, libertarians believe that the constraints that the Constitution places on the federal government from interfering with our individual rights protect all of us, regardless of how we identify. (Many of us had no problem with gay marriage long before Democrats came around to the same position.)

But to base your entire political outlook on one issue that is such a relatively small piece of the political pie is to ignore a whole slew of more significant ones.

As mentioned, the gay "right" that was in public debate the longest in recent years was gay marriage. I use quotation marks to designate it as a right because a right is essentially something that we are born with and that does not impinge upon the rights of others. Having the government officially sanction your decision to make someone your lifelong partner, be it of the same sex or different, doesn't seem to fit the description of a right so neatly. Nevertheless, many libertarians say if we're going to have the government involved in the licensing of marriage in the first place, we can't say which consenting adults we do or don't grant that license to. We are told that conservatives want gays to go back into the closet and that liberals want to see them treated with all the "rights" straight people have. However, the truth is that not all those who identify as Democrats were or are in favor of gay marriage, nor do all Republicans oppose it. While most of this book does not give specific facts to promote an argument, it's too tempting to avoid it now: Pew Research found that in 2017, 40% of Republicans supported gay marriage, while 73% of Democrats did. That means over 25% of Democrats didn't and over a third of Republicans did! Still a clear difference from one side of the aisle to the other, but the issue is not as black-and-white as liberals may believe (or as they would have you believe).

But you don't have to call yourself a liberal because you believe gay people should be allowed to get married. How about not making it a government issue in the first place? Many libertarians ask this question. Why does the government have to sanction heterosexual marriages anyway? Wouldn't it be a lot easier if people could carry out these personal unions with their clergy or create a private contract with a lawyer? Why does the government have to have a say in the matter? Doesn't getting a marriage "license" seem a little ridiculous?

When it comes to gay marriage, we know that there are still prominent Republican politicians who aren't fans. However, their opinions haven't led to anything major getting in the way of gays getting married. In fact, the Supreme Court, in 2015, decided that gays had the right to marry. The majority opinion was even written by Anthony Kennedy, appointed by that evil Republican Ronald Reagan.

But perhaps the heavy hand of the federal government, which liberals only support when it mandates things they like, wasn't really necessary. Times were changing anyway.

Gay marriage had already been legal in thirty-six states. And remember, it was Democrat Bill Clinton who supported the Defense of Marriage Act (which was against gay marriage), and Democrat Barack Obama, as mentioned earlier, who came into office having said he believed that he was okay with civil unions but was opposed to gays getting married. (It was only later that his views "evolved" on the issue.) Just picking a Democrat on election day is not a clear path to furthering gay "rights."

Of course there are other issues relating to gay "rights," but all of them have seen tremendous change in recent years. There are numerous laws that prohibit discrimination in the workplace against gays, lesbians, and transgendered people. The Defense of Marriage Act is dead. Bill Clinton's Don't Ask, Don't Tell policy is gone, too, and the military even got rid of banning transgendered people from serving openly. People who consider themselves part of the LGBTQIA+ community have a lot of things they didn't have just a few years ago.

Other areas where some liberals' goals have not yet been achieved concern not just these LGBTQIA+ issues, but whether private individuals must be compelled to do things against their will. Of course, there is the well-known case about whether a private bakery should be forced to bake a cake for a gay wedding. The Supreme Court ruled that a baker who claimed to hold religious objections to gay marriage did not have to bake the cake. Even some of the court's supposedly liberal justices voted in favor of the baker. What many people might not realize is that the baker didn't refuse to bake a cake for the gay couple. He refused to put the words "support gay marriage" on the cake as well as a logo of an organization that fights for so-called gay rights. Many liberals felt this ruling was not right. But really, what if the cake maker was Jewish and had to make a cake for noted antisemite Louis Farrakhan with the words, "Black Christian Pride" in icing? Extreme analogy, but the point is that if it's your business, you should be entitled to serve or not serve any customers you choose, or only provide products you choose to. Any truly racist or prejudiced business would quickly be outed by customers and lose business or go out of business. Once the government starts mandating that people have to make their product for any cause the customer supports, you've suddenly stopped believing in their right to free speech. This is not a fight for gay "rights." It's a fight for thought control, and any true "liberal" should be against it.

So isn't the "fight" over? It should be, but the LGBTQIA+ movement has now focused increasingly on the alleged mistreatment of transgendered individuals, men and women who identify as the opposite gender from which they were assigned at birth or who have even had surgical or medical treatments to change their bodies. The movement has also focused on everyone else's obligation to recognize the needs of the "non-binary," meaning people that don't identify as either male or female. In both of these cases, we are told what pronouns we must use to correctly refer to these people, even if the pronouns are plural to refer to individuals (they/them) or complete gibberish (ze/zir). Some on the left now want children to be able to decide what gender they are and even be able to have "gender-affirming" surgeries or puberty-blocking medicines.

This is too far for many Americans, including sensible liberals, who are still resistant to things like permanently changing a child's body based on what could easily be a temporary whim, allowing adults who are biologically male to use the same restroom as young girls, or letting biological males compete against women in sporting events.

I can't imagine what it must be like to feel you are not the gender that you are. However, that doesn't mean everyone else must have their privacy, safety, and comfort taken away, or that children should be making their own irreversible medical decisions that they will one day regret.

All that being said, is it then worth putting someone in office because of their stance on one issue, ignoring all others? Many liberals think so, which causes us to get elected officials who ride into office because they happen to be vocal about LGBTQIA+ "rights." Once there, they don't actually make lives better for members of the LGBTQIA+ "community." All they do is further grow the size of government, which is the real danger we should all be focusing on. Big government makes us all worse off, a fact which I will continue to discuss in later chapters. When considering this, liberals' opinion on such a relatively minor issue of LGBTQIA+ "rights" seems all the less important.

The work of the LGBTQIA+ "rights" advocates is pretty much over. Gays and lesbians are all over our screens and fill our cultural institutions. Even the transgendered make appearances in the media from time to time as well. It's time for one-issue devotees to stop seeing this as a reason to always vote for the person with a D next to their name and look at more important considerations.

They Are Preoccupied with Abortion and Women's "Rights"

*"It's not an exaggeration to say women will die —
poor women, women of color will die — because
these Republican legislatures in these various
states who are out of touch with America are telling
women what to do with their bodies."— Kamala
Harris, future Vice President, at the time a United
States senator, after several states banned abortion
as early as the first trimester, with exceptions
including when the woman's life is in danger*

Some liberals also align themselves as leftists because their perceived plight of American women drives their entire political outlook. These issues range from abortion and free contraception to equal pay and representation in business, media, politics, and math and science fields to sexual harassment and sexism.

Let's start with abortion. Liberals often decry a lack of "reproductive rights," a euphemism if ever there were one. Liberals care about women's right to reproduce? It seems like they actually care about women's desire to *not* reproduce. For many on the left, this misleading phrase is actually code for unrestricted abortion up until the final second of pregnancy. Many on the left also expect this and contraception to be provided "free" courtesy of taxpayers. (You can check out the chapter on health care for why these two items should not involve government nor be paid for, unless voluntarily, by everyone else.)

Strangely, liberals call themselves "pro-choice" on this issue, but don't realize that it's one of the few issues where they actually do believe that people should be given a choice in their actions. When abortion "rights" activists say that no one should tell a woman what to do with her body, it's almost funny. They really don't mean that. After all, legalizing drugs would be letting women (and men) do what they want with their own bodies, but most liberals are not for that. Letting parents choose where to send their children to school would be letting women (and men) do what they want with their own (children's) bodies. Allowing people to sell their own organs as opposed to just donating them would be letting women (and men) do what they want with their own bodies. And perhaps you'll say this next one is a stretch, but I don't think so: Eliminating most regulations and taxes would be allowing women (and men) to do what they want with their bodies because, after all, when you have to work for the government for at least 25% of the year (since your earnings are taken by the government), that's not being able to control your own body. It has become someone else's. We won't even get into the hypocrisy on COVID-19 vaccine mandates from the same people who shout, "My body, my choice!" But again, that's not what abortion "rights" activists really mean. The words being spewed for their cause are truly just rhetoric.

Those on the "other side," if we're going to sharply divide Americans into those two camps, are often referred to as "pro-life." It's prevailing wisdom that most Republicans are pro-life. There are plenty of nuances to that position of course. A pro-lifer can be against abortion regardless of the circumstances, accepting of it if the mother in question was the victim of rape or incest, or okay with it if the mother's life is in danger or if it's early enough in the pregnancy.

On the other hand, most Democrats seem to be on the other side of the fence. Many believe abortion should always be legal. Or some believe that anything in the first one or two trimesters should be okay. As mentioned above, it's a woman's body after all, they claim.

Pro-lifers say, um, no, it's not just the woman's body. There's a fetus's body, too. They say the unborn child has rights, as it's a human being the moment the egg is fertilized. Would it be okay to kill an unwanted baby after it's been delivered? Of course not. So why would it be okay to do so just a few seconds before delivery, merely based on which side of the birth canal it's on?

I personally have been somewhat pro-choice for my whole life but am increasingly uncomfortable with it. I've seen those horrific, graphic pictures. I think we all have. I know that whatever stage that fetus is in, it's a life, and the act of killing it disturbs me. I'm bothered by the idea that once he or she is outside the mother's body, intentionally ending the life of a baby is considered unthinkable, but as some believe, if it's still inside, it's fair game.

Still, that hasn't convinced me that it should be completely illegal on a federal level. I think it's such a tricky issue and I can completely understand both sides. That's why many libertarians believe it should have always been a state issue, which is what happened when Roe v. Wade was overturned by the Supreme Court in 2022. Essentially, the states where most people believe abortion is okay allow it to be legal. States where people are very pro-life make it illegal. Having a one-size-fits-all national policy to ban it or not ban it seems highly unfair and against the Constitution, especially given the divided opinions in the country on this important issue.

Back in 2019, Alabama made news for passing a law that outlawed almost all abortions. My friends on social media posted about how all these white men had decided what a woman could do with her body. I wasn't quite sure what the representatives' race had to do with it. But what was interesting was what the posters didn't mention: The governor who signed the bill, the one who actually made it law? A woman. The elected representatives, those evil white men (and female governor) – who do you think elected them? Men *and* women. These were the elected representatives that women had chosen. Certainly, those representatives' viewpoints on abortion hadn't been secret prior to the election. By and large, this was what Alabama's residents wanted. This was what they believed was right. Liberals in other states should understand that not all women have to have the same viewpoint they do.

Regardless, liberals paint abortion as something everybody must be okay with, or else they must be anti-women. However, 57% of women are either pro-life or believe that abortion should only be "legal in a few circumstances." But liberals don't even consider the position that many Americans find the practice morally reprehensible. You might say, why is it anyone's business whether you have your child aborted? The same reason why anyone has a say in the laws against the murder of a stranger, for instance. Someone is being killed, and just because a mother's body would otherwise be needed to sustain the life of an aborted baby, that doesn't change the fact that you're killing a human. A six-month-old baby would also not survive without an adult to sustain it. That argument just doesn't hold up.

Again, the idea that it's "my body" is a little sketchy. We're not talking about getting a tattoo or a face lift. But liberals don't even think about any option besides it being nationally "legal" or "illegal," not taking into account that maybe dictating morals to an entire nation of 300-plus million people is an incredible intrusion on personal beliefs, religious or otherwise.

There are certainly many states in the U.S. where an abortion is harder or impossible to legally get in the wake of Roe v. Wade being struck down. However, while one may personally not want to be so restricted in their choices, one also needs to respect the views of both men and women in those areas who do not feel abortion is a moral practice. And if I'm a woman who is sexually active, maybe I need to take some responsibility for my actions. Maybe I need to even move to another state where I can do as I please and get an abortion at any time. If I don't want to pack up and move, I may need to take a day off work and cross over into a neighboring state to get my abortion. My "rights" aren't missing – but no one should be obligated to provide me with an abortion clinic that is geographically convenient.

Let's put all that aside for now though. Roe v. Wade was the law of the land for 50 years. Whether Republicans or Democrats were in power for all those decades, not much changed regarding abortion for all that time. President George Bush was pro-life, but abortion didn't suddenly become banned as many liberals feared it would. Other staunch opponents or proponents of abortion have served in all branches of government, and yet the abortion issue remained untouched on a national level. Even during Donald Trump's presidency, Republicans had majorities in both houses of Congress, and the Supreme Court was considered to have a conservative majority. Still, nothing happened to abortion on a national level until after he left office and a case made its way up to the Court. And even now, screaming liberals haven't lost the ability to get abortions in the United States. The court just recognized that it was never a Constitutional right, which even liberal icon Ruth Bader Ginsburg acknowledged. Liberals should realize that it's downright silly to base your entire political philosophy on an ongoing fight for something that doesn't require the effort.

As far as the idea that one's abortion should be free, that's a different issue. It's one thing to say your "right" to an abortion shouldn't be taken from you. It's another to say that someone else needs to pay for it. The reality is that many abortions are paid for, at least in part, by taxpayers. But no, not everyone gets a free abortion on demand, and they shouldn't. That now infringes on other people's right to free expression of religion and ownership of personal property. In other words, people have the right to not have to pay for something with which they disagree, especially on religious grounds. They also have the right to keep their personal property, i.e. the money they earn from working, from being used for what is essentially a charity they don't believe in.

This includes taxpayers funding Planned Parenthood and any other authoritarian programs requiring everyone else to have to pay for your contraception. Just because conservatives don't want to fund Planned Parenthood doesn't mean anyone is prevented from making voluntary contributions. You're welcome to fund it with your own money all you'd like. (See more about socialized medicine in the chapters on Europe, socialism, and health care.)

Aside from abortion, contraception, and calls for taxpayers to fund such services and products, liberals also say that women suffer from other atrocities, including unequal pay, unequal representation in positions of power and in the business, math, and science world, and that they are victims of the great white patriarchy.

Let's start with the so-called pay gap. We're told that men and women earn vastly different amounts for the same jobs. Clearly, discrimination is at work, right? No. Simply put, most of the stated pay gap is the result of men working longer hours, choosing to work in different or more dangerous fields, or having more experience. There is no evidence that any difference in pay is due to women being discriminated against. When the data are adjusted for all these factors, it turns out that women make nearly the same amount for a given job. Any minute difference that remains is probably because men are more likely to do things like push for raises, not because there is some kind of systemic anti-women bias. So when liberals like Vice President Kamala Harris came out with plans to penalize business owners for having some male employees receiving higher salaries that some female employees, and then it turned out that her own campaign was guilty of the very same conduct, the hypocrisy stank.

So why aren't there more female CEOs? While the number of female CEOs has risen over the years, we're still nowhere near a 50-50 split, at least as demonstrated on the Forbes 500. There are many theories out there, but of course none proven. Some say it's because of the great patriarchy which doesn't want to see women rise in power. However, others say that even women don't respond well to other women and prefer to have male bosses. Some say women don't aspire to those positions or push as hard to get them. All may or may not have some kernel of truth. But as I mentioned, we don't have evidence to explain the reason. So jumping to the conclusion that the stereotypes and mistreatment of women that existed in shows like *Mad Men* are what are causing the large number difference isn't justifiable. We have multiple laws in place that prohibit discrimination in the workplace. Companies are encouraged either by various government mandates or by societal pressure to hire more women in positions of power. Unfortunately, these kinds of policies, like Affirmative Action for ethnic minorities, only instill a belief in other employees as well as the candidates themselves that they were hired not for their abilities but for their biological makeup.

Additionally, having a small number of female CEOs out of the Fortune 500 companies does not indicate that women do not hold positions of power in business. Nearly 12 million businesses in this country are owned by women! That's not even including the millions of women who hold executive or higher levels in business. Would it be nice if there were exactly the same number of female CEOs as male CEOs? I'm not sure that matters. It's very possible that women, in general, just aren't pining for such goals or taking the risks and making the hard compromises necessary to reach those goals. That's not an insult to those women – they very well may have other goals in mind besides big paychecks and titles.

In math and science, certainly we associate those fields with more men than women. Various studies on the subject show that women can be just as good at math and science as men can be. So why do we see fewer women in those fields? Surely, it's either because of discrimination, or society telling those girls they must be stay-at-home moms, right? What if women in general, as compared to men in general, just weren't as interested in math and science? What if the biological differences between the two genders in this field had nothing to do with a perceived slight against women's ability, but in fact about personal choice? Are we really going to say there's something wrong with that?

Wait, you say, haven't I heard of the "#metoo" movement? Don't I know about discrimination and sexual harassment?

Of course. We heard about some very high-profile celebrities, most but not all of whom were men, who presumably used their power to force people (most but not all of whom were women) to have sex with them, or to be made, well, very uncomfortable. This must be evidence of the great plight that women in this country go through.

No. It's evidence that people in power, especially men, have the potential to be incredibly manipulative, cruel, and downright gross. But most of the ones who were accused of such acts have either faced criminal charges or had their careers destroyed, sometimes completely as a result of un-proven allegations. The notion that we should believe the accusers at all times seems to not have appeared as ridiculous to many liberals as one might expect, despite revelations about supposed victims such as actor Jussie Smollett, UVA student Jackie Coakley, or Duke Lacrosse Team accuser Crystal Gail Mangum being exposed as complete liars who made their whole stories up.

The entertainment industry in particular is often the subject of complaints regarding the treatment of women. We're told there are so few female directors of major movies, roles only go to young women, actresses are sometimes paid less than their male counterparts, and not enough of the studio exec-utives and writers are women. Even though by all measure-ments, those numbers are improving, they still can be seen as evidence of women's mistreatment. But wait, I'm confused. I thought liberals fight these things. Isn't Hollywood, even its dastardly white men in positions of power, composed overwhelmingly of big-time liberals? Don't they pretty much all support Democrats and liberal causes? Surely the liberal Hollywood men who give big bucks to Democrats are all models of treating women with respect, right? (Uh, besides Harvey Weinstein. Oh, and those other guys accused of misconduct like James Franco, Matt Lauer, Charlie Rose, Russell Simmons, Jeffrey Tambor, Bill Cosby, Louis C.K., Jeremy Piven, Dustin Hoffman, Oliver Stone, Ben Affleck, Roman Polanski, Morgan Freeman, and so on.)

That should tell us something. Calling yourself a "progressive" or a "liberal" doesn't really do anything to improve conditions for women. Voting for Democrats and supporting their causes doesn't either. If Hollywood, the most liberal place on Earth, can't solve the supposed problems it has identified, shouldn't we realize that the left's policies are not the solution?

Women certainly have challenges to face. But by no means are women's "rights" under attack. We know that women can achieve great wealth and success in our country, regardless of their gender, as we have many examples of people that have done exactly that. They have achieved that success with hard work, without making excuses, and sometimes with a little luck – the same way their male counterparts reached those goals.

But even if all this weren't true, voting for a Democrat, or considering yourself a liberal because you believe women have it tough is clearly not the way to go. Take a look at a so-called champion of women, Hillary Clinton. Shirts emblazoned with the slogan, "I'm with her" were worn by many liberals when she ran for president. She was supposed to be the face of the women's movement, the one who not only represented so much promise, but who had fought and would fight for women's issues. But Hillary Clinton has been no friend of women. She might talk the talk, but she hasn't walked the walk. When her husband was accused by multiple women of sexual harassment and even outright rape, Hillary allegedly created a "war room" designed to discredit and destroy those women, even sending her security agents to these women to threaten them. Her "charitable" foundation has accepted tons of support from countries like Saudi Arabia that have atrocious records on women's rights, and where oppression of women really exists. While in office, she was responsible for the sale of billions of dollars' worth of weapons from those countries. Yet her attacks on politicians who supposedly were a danger to women's rights always seemed to focus on those here in America who maybe just weren't pro-choice.

Maybe you say, so what if she took money from horrible places? Who would refuse a donation? Well, would a women's advocate do that? No. Her "accomplishments" on women's issues are pretty much nonexistent other than being one, and the actions she has taken makes any non-liberal question whether she has been an advocate for women at all.

We've had liberals in office for hundreds of years. Society has improved for women not because of elected Democrats but because it has evolved for the better, and will continue to do so, in the absence of activist hyperbole and government mandates.

They Worship Obama

"I have to tell you, you know, it's part of reporting this case, this election, the feeling most people get when they hear Barack Obama's speech. My, I felt this thrill going up my leg. I mean, I don't have that too often." — Chris Matthews, former MSNBC political commentator

know this will sound offensive, but many liberals don't have much actual basis for their beliefs. Their liberalism may have even appeared out of nowhere when a rising young star arose from the ashes at the conclusion of the Bush presidency.

Barack Obama is and was appetizing to the liberal taste bud. He speaks well. He's nice looking, thin, and most importantly, African-American. Half, anyway. He was the perfect opportunity for white liberals to prove how open and accepting they were, and for black liberals to get a likeable member of their "tribe" into the White House. Race wasn't a non-issue, as it should be. It was *the* issue.

One's race, culture, ethnicity, or religion should never be perceived as a negative, of course. But equally, it should not be perceived as a positive. It simply shouldn't matter. A black man does not represent all black people just as I don't represent all Jews. But race did matter. It was a big deal that he would be the first black president. Never mind that his policies would be destructive and unconstitutional. He was black and a good speaker.

So when there was a black president, some people couldn't control their excitement. He was and is treated as a god, some sort of gift from the heavens. Other presidents have received undue worship, but nothing like the way Obama is treated. It's not because he promised grand changes in the American way of life (and has delivered on some, for better or worse). Bill Clinton promised change, too. It's got almost nothing to do with his Obama's actual beliefs (aside from the fact that he is on the left, of course). It's because, to those non-black Americans who get excited because a friendly black man or woman has entered the room and presents a chance to demonstrate one's cultural awareness and lack of racist thought, Obama fulfilled that fantasy a thousand-fold. He is that cool black guy who white liberals want to be friends with. He is their way of making themselves feel less guilty for past racism committed by other people who shared their skin color.

These same worshippers went gaga during his inauguration. It became *the* event of the beginning of the millennium. People were in tears. They paid exorbitant hotel prices, took off time from work, and pulled their kids out of school, in order to *be* there when the king was crowned.

People who were not into politics or fashion suddenly followed the Obama family like admirers of royalty would. They would discuss what *Michelle* was wearing, or what Obama's kids' favorite subjects in school were. They would gush on a public kiss between the new president and the first lady, as though they were part of this magical, majestic clan.

When has the American public ever so closely fawned over a U.S. president? Sure, the relatively attractive or well-spoken ones (Clinton and Kennedy) do get their share of attention, but never like this.

Yes, it was "historic" to have the first African-American man in the presidency. After the long years of mistreatment in slavery and the era of Jim Crow, it signaled something that was, at the very least, indicative of the change in American perspectives over time. But getting behind someone simply because his skin color is similar to the skin color of other people who used to get treated horribly is an embarrassingly silly reason to support a candidate. How about doing your homework and finding out what will really help the country? Pick the man or woman that will do that. Not the one with the right hue.

Having a man to idolize in the Oval Office certainly solidified any liberal's existing political viewpoint. But for those apolitical Americans, those on the fence, or those whose own lives were so vacant that they could be easily led any direction by an appealing personality, Barack Obama has been a reason in and of himself for liberals to be liberal. If Americans of all stripes could successfully take their attachment to personalities out of their politics, they would be able to focus on issues that are truly important.

They Hate Trump

"Here's the thing — if Donald Trump is elected president of the United States, in a kind of historical way, it's exciting because we will see the actual last president of the United States. It just won't work after that." — Actor Johnny Depp

Adhering to the liberal cause based on your obsession with one man is not limited to Barack Obama lovers. Many people consider themselves progressives primarily because of their hatred of President Donald Trump.

If you've been paying any attention to the rest of this book, you'd realize that as a fan of small and efficient government, I have plenty of criticism for Trump. I still would have greatly preferred him over Joe Biden, of course. But despite Biden's massive failures when it came to the southern border, for instance, Trump's own Border Patrol policies included failing to swiftly process detainees, leading to serious over-crowding and unsanitary conditions. His views on free trade, among other aspects of economics, are not typically conservative viewpoints. His expansion of federal spending is not conservative whatsoever. His view on the role of government in our lives is contrary to mine. So I voted for the Libertarian Party candidate in that election, since I felt Trump would not be good and Biden would be terrible.

At the same time, there's no denying that the so-called Trump Derangement Syndrome, where one's loathing for him erodes all traces of logic or objectivity, really does exist. Liberals paint him as an evil white supremacist. Sure, he has said things that could be construed as offensive to immigrants from Mexico, as well as to women and Muslims. His seemingly abusive use of power to damage political rivals, like Joe Biden, could be seen as unethical and arguably illegal. The federal government's handling of the COVID-19 pandemic while he was in office left a lot to be desired by many. And the so-called "insurrection" on January 6th of 2021 remains a focal point for those on the left.

But in reality, after one term in office, none of the horror stories actually came true. Public education was not "destroyed," rising sea levels didn't engulf coastal cities worldwide, Muslims and Mexicans were not cleansed from American streets, and "trans" people were not relegated to prison camps. His reviled rhetoric and policies about illegal immigrants, for instance, were often not that different from those of Barack Obama and Hillary Clinton, for whom I also did not and would not vote.

No matter what he did or continued to do, the left attacked Trump. When he tried to end or reduce American intervention in foreign countries, the supposedly anti-war left managed to criticize his actions. After the violent Charlottesville rally, the media told us he was referring to neo-Nazis when he said there were "good people on both sides." Listening to the whole quote, which the mainstream media wouldn't do, you can clearly see he was saying that people that were *peacefully protesting against the removal of Confederate statues* were "fine people." You may disagree that such a position is "fine," but his actual meaning is far different than what the media continues to propagate.

The left also attacked him for supposedly colluding with Russia to win the 2016 election. The Mueller Report, which was the FBI's analysis of Russian interference in the 2016 election, somehow gave both conservatives and liberals the ammunition they felt they needed. It's perfectly reasonable to question Trump's involvement in the effort to get Russian operatives to dig up dirt on his opponent, but to say definitively that Trump "stole the election" or that Russia "handed him the win" is ludicrous. The evidence that any of this mattered in his win is simply not there. That doesn't excuse his alleged behavior. It just means we need to all take a step back and not hyperventilate. We're not talking about the actual manipulation of voting results or election tampering.

We're talking about an alleged attempt at getting more information to voters in order to come out ahead. Whether the information was always accurate or obtained properly is another question. And yet, would any of us say that all the information voters had before the supposed Russian meddling was accurate either? Election ads were otherwise unbiased and never misleading?

His handling of the pandemic was also widely criticized. The media said he wasn't taking COVID-19 "seriously." He was blamed for not having enough testing, overpromising about when the virus would go away, not endorsing masks, not investing enough in the Centers for Disease Control, not having a national strategy, not saving people's jobs, and the list goes on and on. People actually said he had "blood on his hands."

And he certainly said some ill-advised remarks. But when Trump was in office, vaccines were fast-tracked through the FDA, even though prominent Democrats like Kamala Harris said she wouldn't take the vaccine since it was developed under Trump. Later in office, she wondered why Americans were slow to be vaccinated. And once he was out of office, the virus didn't get under control as Biden seemed to indicate it would. Roughly the same number of people died from COVID-19 in Trump's last year in office as in Biden's first, and Biden had multiple vaccines to work with.

When it comes to the "Insurrection," the left still holds Trump accountable for the violent actions of those that actually entered the Capitol that day. They ignore the fact that while he certainly did continue to claim the election was stolen, he told protestors to remain peaceful. But those who scream, "Insurrection!" seemed to have no problem with Hillary Clinton claiming the 2016 election was stolen, or that there was violence across the country immediately after her defeat as well. Furthermore, what kind of insurrection is done by people who are mostly unarmed, and many of whom are actually let into the building by security?

Again, Trump has done and said plenty of things I don't support. While I may be accused of "what-aboutism," let's not pretend that Trump is the first president to be involved in scandals. Obama, loved by Trump haters, oversaw an IRS that targeted conservatives, failed and then deceived on the Benghazi mission, collected phone records from the Associated Press, allowed American weapons to go to Mexican drug dealers ("Fast and Furious"), and the list goes on. We just don't hear about those mess-ups much because it's Barack, not Donald.

Even if you don't buy any of this line of thinking, what then? So you believe he's slime – does that mean you should define yourself as a liberal because one Republican president was immoral in your eyes? You should ignore all historical evidence, economics, ethics, and the Constitution as long as you put someone in office who has a "D" next to their name?

It's perfectly fine to be opposed to Trump. Plenty of conservatives and Republicans are, too. And it's even okay to think he's sometimes buffoonish, offensive, and possibly guilty of illegal or immoral actions. But to think he's a monster and his opponent in his first run for office was a goddess from heaven is to not be aware of reality and to be fully enveloped in a cocoon of delusion. Disliking Trump is a terrible reason to be a liberal.

They Hate Bush

"If you believe in the seamless mutuality of government and big business, come out and say it! There is a dictionary definition, one word that describes that toxic blend. You're a fascist! Get them to print you a T-shirt with fascist on it! You, sir, have no place in a government of the people, by the people, for the people." — Keith Olbermann, former MSNBC host, referring to President George W. Bush

A similar phenomenon happened with former president George W. Bush. For the record, I'm also not a fan of his. Under his leadership, the size of the federal government grew tremendously. Of course, you could say the same for nearly every other president in US history, especially during the 20th and 21st centuries. However, Bush was also the man in the White House on 9/11 and chose to pursue the Iraq War presumably to find weapons of mass destruction, which drove many lefties to further self-identify as liberals.

My opinions are very strong when it comes to federal spending and government overreach, but primarily when we're talking domestically. When it comes to wars and the international actions of our military-industrial complex, I'm somewhat less passionate. I know that's sacrilegious to say as a libertarian, but I'm coming around. I also hear very different opinions from strong voices within the libertarian movement with regard to our international presence overall, and whether the Iraq War was justified. Seeing the loss of human life and the overwhelming financial burden that these constant wars have brought us has made me doubt that most of them have made us any safer.

But liberals who despise Bush generally view him as a far greater villain than his successor, Barack Obama. And yet, despite promises to the contrary, Barack Obama continued in the path of Bush. The operation of the ultra-secretive Guantanamo Bay military detention center in Cuba, singled out for alleged mistreatment and torture of enemy combatants who are, some say, being detained unlawfully, was not shut down. While scaling down our presence in places like Iraq, Obama also continued our military intervention campaigns across the world, and even ramped up the use of military force in engagements outside of Iraq, such as Afghanistan. Under him, the government also collected data without a warrant on American citizens not accused or necessarily involved in any terrorist activities, just as it had under Bush. But Bush is the one who gets the lion's share of the venom from liberals, not Obama.

Bush also was the villain in the oft-repeated refrain, "Bush lied, people died." Many of those who loathed him the most claimed that he knew there were no WMDs in Iraq but chose to pursue the war anyway for any number of bad reasons. They said it was because he wanted oil for the U.S. He wanted a scapegoat for 9/11. He wanted to misdirect American's attention from domestic troubles. He wanted to get money for military-contracted Haliburton, which he and his cronies somehow profited from. He wanted to continue his father's unsuccessful venture in that part of the world. Rarely did they just say that they believed he was simply wrong. However, most Democrats in office at the time also supported the war in Iraq, but of course Bush gets all the blame.

And yet when Obama kept troops in Iraq until ultimately replacing them with some vaguely labeled peacekeepers, kept Guantanamo Bay open, initiated or continued conflicts in other regions, and even kept some of the same top Bush-era defense and military personnel in place, most supposedly anti-war liberals suddenly went hush-hush in their protests. Why?

Because liberals just hate Bush. He's from Texas, and liberals seem to believe any conservative from Texas is double-evil.

Bush did fine in college but has been ridiculed for being an idiot because he's no world class speaker by any standard. And despite his international military policies being very similar to his conversely idolized successor, Bush is the Devil incarnate to liberals, and enough reason for many to be liberals in the first place.

He's also been out of office for a while now, so progressives should get over it. He's definitely not a good reason to be a liberal.

Some Are Just Immoral

"May your children all die from debilitating, painful and incurable diseases." — Allan Brauer, communications chair of the Democratic Party of Sacramento County to Ted Cruz staffer Amanda Carpenter

That's right. There are people out there that are liberal because they just don't have a sense of right and wrong.

While classical liberalism was all about freedom and keeping the government from treading on that freedom, modern liberalism is all about having the government use force to impose the will of a certain vocal group of the population upon the less vocal ones, who perhaps are often busy raising families and holding jobs. The heavy hand of the government, the use of force at the point of a gun to go far beyond just protecting the life, liberty, and property of citizens, doesn't seem to faze liberals. They want what they want and they aren't ashamed to force what they want on other people.

And isn't forcing your opinions on other people immoral? We're not talking about pretty much universally agreed upon norms (in the Western world, anyway) like saying that murder and theft should be punishable by incarceration (although many on the left are walking away from that notion, too). We're talking about the idea that if you believe certain groups of people need some form of assistance, rather than you stepping up and giving that money to those people, you believe that that money should be actually *taken* from people to fund the cause you believe in. We're talking about giving money to an environmental program, an impoverished country, a sector of the working class, a racial group, or an industry, all because that's the one *you* happen to believe in. It's not just giving of your *own* resources but believing that because you (or enough of you) believe in supporting a cause, therefore everyone must be *required* to.

Of course liberals have long ago rationalized that if the government doesn't force citizens to help each other, its citizens won't. We'll get to that in another chapter that talks about the actual history of voluntary actions before government pushed its way in.

But the bottom line is that is that it's wrong for anyone to think that other people should be hauled off to jail (that's what happens if you don't pay your taxes after all) for not supporting a cause that someone else believes in. It's wrong to force people to work at a job for months out of the year just to produce the money that some liberal decided the government can take from them, all in order to fund the government that is favored by that liberal.

When people say Democrats are so kind and generous compared to Republicans, they somehow are confused about reality. When you say you want to give money to help a cause, but it's someone else's money, that's not kind and generous! It's immoral. Plain and simple.

Aside from taking your time and money by force for their own purposes, leftists are also immoral in countless other ways: getting violent criminals back out on the streets early which puts innocent people in danger, implementing Affirmative Action (racism by a different name) and Critical Race Theory, taking guns away from otherwise defenseless citizens, indoctrinating young schoolchildren with their politics and sexual beliefs, supporting mob violence to achieve social justice goals, pushing for abortion up to the last moment of pregnancy, and labeling words they don't like as "hate speech" so as to criminalize them. Of course there are many others.

If only liberals realized the true lack of ethics that they exhibit, maybe they would stop being so entrenched in the evil of the left.

They Live in Fantasy Land

"You shouldn't speak until you know what you're talking about. That's why I get uncomfortable with interviews. Reporters ask me what I feel China should do about Tibet. Who cares what I think China should do? I'm a [expletive] actor! They hand me a script. I act. I'm here for entertainment. Basically, when you whittle everything away I'm a grown man who puts on makeup." — Actor Brad Pitt, who hasn't shied away from sharing his opinion on politics in the years since making this statement

There are some people in this country who have the knowledge, background, life experience, and genuine desire for good, to whom many of us turn for their opinions. But there are far too many liberals who have arrived at their political opinions because they are completely out of touch with the real world. This includes celebrities, the ultra-wealthy, college students, and career politicians.

Imagine if there were someone whose entire way of living was to record songs in a studio, or dress up and play pretend? What if that person spent much of their existence being paid such exorbitant sums of money that they could survive for long periods of time without even finding work, and maybe even live in a mansion with an ocean view, drive luxurious cars, have the ability to travel without worrying about cost, and were surrounded by assistants, managers, security guards, and agents who catered to their every whim, both physical and emotional, not to mention millions of adoring fans? Surely, such a person would not be the best person to seek opinions on how the world works or should work for the rest of us, right? But that is exactly what happens.

Yes, as we've heard, Hollywood is dominated by the left, and being a celebrity or being steered by what celebrities say about politics is yet another bad reason some people are liberals. Many celebrities never have held a "normal" job, or it's been so long since those days as a waiter or waitress that they've forgotten what it was like. Paying more taxes, higher gas prices, or inflation-boosted prices may not seem as big of a deal when you haven't put your blood, sweat, and tears into your wages, or when you haven't had to wonder if you can afford your daughter's tuition, let alone the next meal.

There will always be more cash delivered hand over fist for the next TV show, movie, or musical release.

So it's no surprise that most celebrities are big time liberals. Sure, there are the rare conservative celebrities like Clint Eastwood, John Voight, Arnold Schwarzenegger, and Mel Gibson, but most of the biggest names of the day – the very people who have the least connection with reality due to the lives they live – are the ones who are Democrats. Is that a coincidence?

What does that say about the causes they support? If you had a political party and it was really popular among 5-year-olds, what would that suggest about the political party? It's probably not the most worthwhile cause to support because its believers have limited understandings of society. If you take a group of people who live in this unreal bubble, completely insulated from the real world by their fawning handlers and the public, as well as being physically removed from the hassles of everyday life by their wealth and fame, and the vast majority of these people supported a cause or a political party, wouldn't that make you wonder about the fundamental traits of the party and ideals they support?

So clearly there are reasons celebrities are overwhelmingly liberal. Further driving them to the left is the fact that not only are they out of touch with reality, but that they are not hearing any other points of view. That's covered in another chapter in this book, but it certainly deserves mention specifically in this one. Celebrities are friends with other celebrities, and with bigwigs in show business. Hearing a point of view that goes contrary to the typical Hollywood line pretty much doesn't happen and may in fact be even less common because of the fear of reprisal and blacklisting that could go on.

Of course there are also rich Americans who are not famous, but still align themselves as liberals for all the wrong reasons. There are disagreements about whether the rich (and how that is defined) tend to be more liberal or conservative, but the results are not what one would expect. It's not a simple case where we can say those evil fat cats wanting to decide for themselves what to do with their stuff (how selfish!) are all Republicans.

But regardless, let's think about how out of touch some wealthy are, and how their political choices are therefore not on the same page as reality. The Warren Buffets or George Soroses of this world, for instance, or even the ultra-rich man or woman with a fraction of their wealth but who lives in a nice house and hasn't actually cleaned his or her own toilet in decades, probably don't have a real solid grasp on what life is like for most Americans, whether it's a kid living in South Central L.A. or one in a decent suburb of Chicago. They don't know what it's like for someone just breaking into the middle class whose gardening business is being hampered by excessive regulations and fees that the Buffets and Soroses of this world promote as ways to "protect" the same little guy.

At the opposite end of the age and wealth spectrum, but somehow still in the same political realm exist college kids. Studies show they are predominantly liberal, which may be a function of their age or their indoctrination by high school teachers and college professors (discussed in an earlier chapter). But what do college kids know about, well, anything? Okay, I might turn to a college kid to show me how to stream a video on my smart phone. But beyond that? It's a similar principle to the one regarding celebrities and the ultra-wealthy. These are people who haven't lived in the real world. Most have not had a real job (i.e. one where the government takes its cut or strangles productivity through excessive regulation) or started a business. Like those discussed in the chapter about the misinformed, college kids only know what's being fed to them on social media and through their educators. They have clearly become liberals for all the wrong reasons (not that there are any right reasons).

Finally, we have the career politicians. What's the best way for a politician to get re-elected? Give stuff away! After years of doing so, you forget (or ignore) the fact that what you're doing is wrong (see the Big Four mentioned earlier). You've probably long since stopped checking (or more likely, never did) if your policies are having a beneficial effect or negative effect. After so long in your cushy government job, you forget what it's like to get up early to feed the kids and get them to a crappy public school and then to not be able to find a better job because of the onerous government policies in place that have increased unemployment.

No, if you're going to arrive at a political opinion, or if you expect me to respect your beliefs, you need to at least come from a place of understanding. Get real.

They Are Jealous

"I think when you spread the wealth around it's good for everybody." — Barack Obama, 44th President of the United States of America

One of the issues that drives liberals, especially those that aren't wealthy, is envy. They don't like that some people in life have ended up on the more "fortunate" side of the economic spectrum.

For whatever reason, some Americans have a lot of stuff. But most didn't win the lottery and aren't trust fund babies. They didn't steal it or take advantage of the "evils of capitalism" to acquire it. Most of them worked hard to get what they have. But that's not information most liberals know or care about. They see that some people are luckier than they are, and they think that's unfair.

Now many of us on all political spectrums are unhappy with our lots in life, especially when it comes to our job, career, or financial situation. Those that blame themselves (in other words, take responsibility) and make a plan to improve their lot in life don't tend to vote for the guy with the capital D next to his name. But once you start thinking that the only reason your job path is limited is that somebody else took advantage of you or the system, you're on the path to voting for the progressive.

So what's the only solution to jealousy? Clearly, those people described above have parents who never sat them down and told them to appreciate what they have, and not resent others for what they have, or to work hard to go after their goals and never stop. That's one reason why jealousy doesn't appear in many people who are less fortunate. But for liberals, they never had that upbringing. So jealousy is one of their biggest driving forces.

Liberals seek to "level the playing field" or make the so-called rich "pay their fair share." "Spreading the wealth" is not a new concept, but its widespread acceptance as a religion is yet another explanation of why so many liberals are liberal. Primarily through taxes, regulations, and entitlements, liberals seek to get some of the wealth from the haves and pass it on to the have-nots. (We'll get into this in the chapter on capitalism.)

Robin Hood may have been a fictional folk hero, but the rich people he stole from in the stories (and the historical background they were based on) weren't working in a free market, where they earned their loot from innovation or providing people with a valued good or service at an acceptable price. They were mostly robber barons, or families with connections to nobility or the king, who could therefore accumulate wealth through nefarious means, including the force of violence.

Interestingly though, liberals don't seem to have any problem with certain wealthy people, as long as they have the right politics. George Soros, Warren Buffet, and Jeff Bezos get a pass from the left. Elon Musk did, too, before he started advocating for free speech. But the much maligned Koch brothers have long been accused of being some secretive machine for evil lurking in the shadows behind any movement deemed politically "conservative" in nature. In fact, Charles and his late brother David have tended to support causes which are truly free-market ideas, not big-government-Republican party ones. They also are ideologically consistent, fighting against laws or subsidies that would involve an expansion of the government's tentacles into the lives of citizens. Ironically or not, the Koch brothers' companies would have actually benefited financially from many of those government handouts that they fought against. In addition, they have supported causes that no one on the left talks about when the Kochs' names come up, such as criminal justice reform. They have also been quite generous when it comes to charity.

In fact, most of the wealthy in the United States, despite what MSNBC and the *Huffington Post* may imply, have not killed or subjugated anyone to rack up their piles of gold coins. When jealous citizens vote for the heavy hand of government to seize the fortune of others to pay for their own desires, that's not only immoral, but it's detrimental to the very people it aims to please. When money is funneled through government, it is poorly managed, misused, and utilized ineffectively. When those rich people, of whom liberals are jealous (or whom rich liberals despise on *behalf* of their poorer brethren – see the chapter on guilt) spend their money on homes, cars, or fancy trips, that creates or sustains other areas of the economy, whether it's real estate or tourism. You don't have to buy into "trickle-down economics" to understand this either. The more the envious keep their filthy hands *off* the rightful property of others, the more opportunity there is for all of us to reach higher financial status as well. When you hear about an evil Republican giving "tax cuts for the rich," stop and think, why would this be bad? Isn't it a good thing when we forcibly take *less* of our citizens' money, no matter who they are? Shouldn't we be looking for opportunities to give tax cuts to everyone? But the jealous liberals don't believe that. They want what other people have to be taken away, because they've decided those people "have enough."

One area the jealous often focus on is the "inequality" of the income gap. They feel that as the rich get richer, the poor get poorer. The truth is that while there certainly is a gap between the amount of income possessed by the rich and the poor in America, it is not only exaggerated or misunderstood in the media -- it shouldn't matter in the first place. For one thing, it's wrong to blindly assume that income differences happen because something is inherently unfair, that the rich lucked into their wealth, or that the poor are that way because of "lack of opportunity" or discrimination. Second, so what if there's a gap? The alternative, as we've seen in examples around the world throughout history is that *everybody* is poorer. In the U.S., even our "poor" are wealthier than the poor in other countries. But capitalism (which is certainly not unhindered currently; see the capitalism chapter) has allowed people throughout history to become better off financially. Not just the rich – everyone. Communism and its other more innocuous-seeming counterparts tend to make people (other than the well-connected) poorer, and yes, to reduce the income gap. I'd rather have a society where there are people who have way more money than I do in exchange for having the opportunity to be better off financially myself. I'm okay with people having more success than me. Progressives should be too.

Along with being jealous, some liberals are that way because they have failed in their pursuit of the American Dream. Whether by sheer luck (or lack thereof), lack of knowledge, or lack of diligence, not everyone in the United States who wishes to start a thriving business, have a loving two-parent family, and own a home with a white picket fence will attain those goals. In fact, 25% of Americans say that the American Dream is out of reach.

Many of us don't know how to attain those facets of the American Dream, and many of us don't bother to put in the work to get them. I know I, for one, give up or get disheartened when something I put a lot of effort doesn't go my way. Still, we're told that those that work incredibly hard and know how to face rejection or disappointment can succeed.

But what happens when the old pull-yourself-up-by-the-bootstraps mantra only makes your boots tighter? What happens when you have done everything you can (or convinced yourself that you have), and fate doesn't deal you any favors?

It's only natural to start questioning ourselves, our abilities, our life plans, and our futures. We wonder, will we ever reach those dreams? Is the idea that you can have anything in America if you just work hard enough for it just a lie we tell children so that they go after their goals without fear?

This is when some people decide to become liberals. Instead of looking inward, instead of facing the hardship by asking tough questions of themselves, and instead of making hard decisions about how to proceed, they look outward. They blame the system. They figure that it doesn't actually work as planned, that people can't achieve their dreams just by sheer diligence. And once they're convinced of that, they decide what the answer is: government must step in. It must ensure things like a "fair" wage, good health care, a financial safety net, an affordable home loan, and so on. Government, they reason, will fill in the gaps where their own luck did not. If we can't have that white picket fence and manicured lawn because home loans are too hard to get, well then good old Uncle Sam should step in and make it possible. If our job doesn't provide the means for the health care we seek, then we need government to step in and make it so. If we're out of work because our latest get-rich-quick scheme was neither quick nor made us rich, then government needs to step in and pay us "unemployment."

But jealousy and being upset with your lot in life is yet another dumb reason to be a liberal. Life is not perfect any-where on Earth. Capitalism may be the best economic sys-tem there has ever been, but that doesn't mean everyone gets rich and gets what they want (especially when our current version of capitalism is already so hindered by government intervention). When government steps in to fill the holes in our lives that we had hoped our dreams would, in the end we're left in an even bigger hole like the one we're in now — massive debt tied to inflation that makes our money worth less and less, a huge regulatory burden that makes getting us affordable and quality goods more and more difficult, and reaching dreams for everyone becomes all the less likely.

They Have Visions of Western Europe

"You go to Scandinavia, and you will find that people have a much higher standard of living, in terms of education, health care and decent paying jobs." — Bernie Sanders (D-VT), United States Senate

Most Americans have never been out of the United States, let alone to western Europe. It's expensive, and travel there is a luxury that most Americans cannot afford. Or perhaps they just choose not to spend their hard-earned money there.

But there are a lot of rich liberals in the U.S. who go to Europe and fall in love with it. They see historic buildings, art museums filled with names like Da Vinci and Michelangelo, and chic dishes that will get them lots of "likes" on social media. Don't get me wrong -- I like traveling to Europe, too, but I don't come back home and wonder why the United States can't be more like it.

Liberal Americans learn that many of these western European countries have "free" health care, convenient public transportation, few mass shootings, and a near absence of visibly homeless people on the street. Certainly, these are all things an (uninformed) American would envy. They instantly start to compare this clean, beautiful, peaceful way of life with that of the United States.

And what do they learn? Western European countries often have high tax rates, and their governments provide more services and often have even more regulation than the United States federal government. And yet their people seem happier, and life seems easier. While one could argue that their right to free speech is not what ours is, they do have religious and sexual freedoms. It even seems like there's less of a gap between rich and poor in many of these countries than back at home.

So clearly America should be more like Europe! American government should operate in an even more hands-on approach than it does in an ever increasingly interventionist mode currently in the States.

But that's where they're wrong. In the overregulated, overtaxed, and over safety-netted societies in Western Europe, not all is wonderful. Economic growth there is limited by burdensome regulations. It's often a difficult or impossible task to start a competitive business given all the restrictions and barriers to entry. That means producers and servicers have fewer competitors, prices are higher, and output is inferior.

With "free" health care comes problems, too, as discussed in a later chapter. Long lines and waits of months or years for lifesaving or life-extending procedures make the fantasy no longer enticing. Plus, how often do medical innovations come out of Europe? What's the incentive to create some new product if you can't reap the reward of all your research and development, or even pay back those debts?

We talked about how liberals are wrongly against the income gap in a previous chapter. In fact, many progressives look to Europe as an ideal for where the income gap is smaller. As discussed, we've seen that in societies with capitalistic tendencies group A may become more socioeconomically distant from group B, but in time, both A and B get progressively wealthier than both counterparts would in a less free nation. In other words, who cares if there's a smaller gap between rich and poor there, if our poor and rich are both better off than theirs?

Plus, look at the standard of living in Europe versus here in the U.S. You know how many "poor" people in the U.S. own TVs and cell phones? Our homes are bigger, and we have more stuff. You can thank a less regulated economy, lower tax rates (although not in all cases), and the entrepreneurial spirit for that.

Furthermore, in many cases, western European countries don't even live up to the ideal of a democratic socialist utopia that many liberals believe. In Scandinavia, wealth inequality is actually worse than it is in the United States, despite the fact that taxes are generally higher there. Sweden's public education is ranked as worse than ours, and Norway and Denmark only slightly better. Homelessness is on the rise throughout Europe and is about the same in many European countries as it is in the United States, in some cases even worse. Switzerland, meanwhile, is remarkably capitalist and therefore not talked much about by American liberals. It also has an amazing educational system, low taxes, and low income inequality. Other western European countries are increasingly moving away from destructive big-government policies. There has been a trend in some of them toward lowering taxes, reducing regulation, and privatization.

If liberals love Europe so much, they should move there. But voting for policies of bigger government in the United States in the hopes of getting government-mandated three-hour siestas is detrimental to what this country is all about, and what's best for its people. Loving Europe is no excuse for being a liberal.

They Are Tribalists

"White folks was in the caves while we [blacks] was building empires... We built pyramids before Donald Trump ever knew what architecture was ... we taught philosophy and astrology and mathematics before Socrates and them Greek homos ever got around to it." — Black "leader" Reverend Al Sharpton

As I stated in the introduction, I'm Jewish, at least when it comes to "ethnicity." (I'm not particularly religious.) While there have been and still are some big names in conservative and libertarian politics who are or were born Jewish (Ben Shapiro, Dennis Prager, Ayn Rand, Milton Friedman, and Barry Goldwater, for instance), there is no question that Jews predominately tend to be lefties.

In fact, you don't need statistics (though the references section provides links to them) to know that most people who label themselves as ethnic minorities in the United States vote for Democrats, too. African-Americans, and to a somewhat lesser degree, Latinos, vote for the liberal candidates, time and time again.

We're told that one of the big reasons for this is that for a long time, ethnic minorities in the United States were truly treated unequally, to say the least. Whether it was Jews, blacks, Latinos, Chinese, Japanese, or Native Americans, they've all been the victims of prejudice. (So were Irish and Italians, but apparently liberals don't count them because today they're considered "white.")

However, the terrible prevalence of racism and prejudice that existed in the past is not a true obstacle to success and a happy life for most minorities nowadays. Racism no longer stands in the way of someone getting a job, a promotion, admission to a university (unless they're white or Asian), or a fair trial. The data just don't keep up the myth that the left has created.

We are led to believe that Democrats are and have always been the champions of "civil rights." Republicans, however, actually played a big part in the past in the advancement of the equal rights of all, and the role of Democrats has been exaggerated. Historical events where Democrats actively worked against equality have long been ignored.

But that's a moot point. We're not in the '60s now. Sure, laws have changed, but attitudes regarding prejudice have changed, too. Poll taxes, laws banning interracial marriage, and separate facilities for different races are all things of the past.

Racism and religious prejudice are not gone, but they certainly are not impediments to success anymore. Life in America in this day and age is for the most part not affected by one's ancestry or skin color.

But minority groups still vote overwhelmingly for Democrats. They still believe that the Democratic Party is the force fighting for "equal rights." Democrats are seen as the guys fighting the evils of a racist country.

It's really quite silly. There's no reason for anyone to be peddling that tired story anymore. But it's even more ridiculous to listen to it and accept it as truth. People need to look beyond rhetoric and emotions when it comes to their ethnic origins, and toward issues that really matter.

What about the supposedly racist criminal justice system? More blacks in prison than whites doesn't mean the system is racist. In fact, most of the racial disparities we can find in statistics related to criminal justice do not require us to conclude that those disparities are actually due to racism. There are a lot more men in prison than women, but no one would argue that the system is sexist against men. If a larger percentage of men are shot by police than women, does that mean police are prejudiced against males? Of course not. The same principle applies to race. There are many factors at play, surely, but liberals always assume discrimination must be the culprit.

There are indeed racist cops. There are certainly disparities along racial lines that can be found across our country when it comes to arrest rates, police searches, conviction percentages, and so on. That doesn't mean that's why one ethnic group may have more run-ins with law enforcement or more cells in America's prisons. Police brutality or excessive use of force is certainly a problem that should be tackled. But it is not one that is stopping most productive, cooperative members of society from advancing in this country.

One talking point that is often brought up as an example is the difference between penalties for cocaine use and crack cocaine use. Laws that penalize crack cocaine use more seriously than its more expensive cousin may seem unfair. But crack is more often associated with other violent behaviors. Just because crack is typically used by poorer drug users who more often tend to be blacks and Latinos, that doesn't mean its harsher penalties are due to racism. Cocaine use by wealthy whites doesn't have the same tendency. (I don't feel either should be illegal, but that's another story.) Further destroying the narrative is the fact that many of these "crackdowns on crack" were spearheaded by African-American Democrats who sought to get rid of drug users in inner cities.

But even if none of this were true – even if you buy into the premise that all of these disparities are due to the fact that white cops, juries, and judges treat blacks and Latinos differently because they simply don't like people with different skin color – what then? Have Democrats helped any of these problems? Or do they just fuel the flames of angry voters? Voting for liberals has not and will never be the answer to fixing an imperfect justice system.

The bigger picture is that we need to stop feeling that we as individuals have no identity, that we are worthless unless we are part of some bigger tribe. I should not be proud because Einstein was a "fellow" Jew. I didn't invent the theory of relativity. He did. The same goes for any ethnicity, religion, or race. You shouldn't be ashamed of your background, but neither should it give you much of which to be proud. Obama should have said his famous line not about American business but about misplaced ethnic pride: "You didn't build that. Somebody else made that happen."

They Hate the Constitution

"The trouble with the theory [of limited and divided government] is that government is not a machine, but a living thing. This is where the living and breathing constitution comes from. It is modified by its environment, necessitated by its tasks, shaped to its functions by the sheer pressure of life." — Woodrow Wilson, 28th President of the United States of America

Our Founding Fathers put their lives at risk by rebelling against the English crown. Many of them would be integral to the process of creating the United States Constitution, the document which set forth the roles of our new and radical government, and the rights of the citizens of the new nation. It was truly a "revolutionary" document, despite the fact that it built upon already existing principles espoused by free-thinking philosophers who inspired it. Its framers had a perspective that most of us don't have, living in a world where the idea of personal liberty and having a voice in one's government was extremely unusual, a time when governments around the world were predominantly authoritarian, and democracies (or republics, as we would eventually become) were few and far between. The guys who wrote the Constitution may have been flawed white men, many of whom didn't live up to the ideals they wrote about, who lived in a time before electricity, automobiles, and showers, but the principles they imbued into the Constitution are timeless.

However, several things about this history have pushed today's liberals to their left-leaning loyalties. One, many of the Founding Fathers owned slaves. Two, the Constitution didn't abolish slavery, and in fact counted enslaved blacks as being worth less than (land-owning) whites. Three, the fact that our nation's government has been involved in many bad things in the past not even including African slavery (Japanese internment, Native American slaughters, Jim Crow laws and segregation, mistreatment of citizens by police, killings in wars overseas, etc.) certainly means that this Constitution our nation is built on is not worth paying much attention to now, they contend. Finally, it was written so long ago, they feel much of it no longer applies, such as a need to bear arms for self-defense and to protect against an overreaching government.

There's an expression for that kind of thinking. We say that disregarding something because parts of it are bad is throwing the baby out with the bath water. There is no excuse for many things the United States government has done, and still continues to do. The fact that many of our Founders had the hypocrisy to preach about liberty while at the same time keeping humans as property is one with which I still struggle. The idea that the Constitution was created at that time and seems to therefore have at least in that aspect a "do as I say, not as I do" mentality is frustrating. And the fact that there were no automatic or even semi-automatic weapons back then might make one wonder just how far the second amendment should extend today.

But that doesn't mean the Constitution is nothing more than a relic from the past. It had its flaws, as did many of those involved in its drafting and enactment. So what though? It's been amended so that those major wrongs have been righted, and yet still retains its all too vital (and all too often ignored) limits on the powers of government in favor of the rights of individuals. We can't say the whole thing is a mess just because it had big issues associated with its creation that we would never accept today.

Furthermore, the Constitution has been violated many, many times over the years, and our great expanse of government today continues to violate the document every second of every day. So just because a lot of atrocities have occurred at the hands of politicians who swore allegiance to the document, that doesn't mean it is the fault of the words on the parchment, whose very meanings have been ignored time and time again.

If anything, we should be reminding our elected leaders and unelected bureaucrats what the Constitution actually says and means, and why the things government does that offend our morality so greatly are actually unconstitutional. Don't blame the Constitution for how it's been abused; blame the abusers. Yet again, liberals have predicated their politics on a misinformed and misguided premise.

Some Just Want to Be "Cool"

"Every Republican's voted for it. Look at what they value and look at their budget and what they're proposing... They're gonna put y'all back in chains." — Joe Biden (before being elected President), presumably intending to demonstrate his solidarity with a predominantly African-American audience

Anyone would be hard-pressed to find a "cool" Republican. The awkward, dorky, old man image that is epitomized by a Mitt Romney or a Mitch McConnell are not exactly few and far between on the left side of the aisle, but they don't seem quite as prevalent as they are on the right. Say what you will about Barack Obama, John F. Kennedy, or Bill Clinton, but as far as politicians go, they certainly exuded some measure of the coolness factor. For better or worse (okay, it's for worse), that's attractive to the general public.

Coolness is also associated with rebelliousness and resistance. That has been perceived to suggest being generally anti-war, anti-police, anti-rich, anti-corporation, and anti-establishment. It also has been perceived to require fighting for the supposed needs of the poor, the non-white immigrant, and the non-white ethnic minority. Rebels are always fighting against something – the "man," society, etc.

Never mind the fact that liberals' professed intentions in all these regards don't correlate to any actual positive results once their chosen representatives are in office. Deportation of illegal immigrants wasn't that much different under Obama vs. Trump, despite what the media tell us. The rate of poverty doesn't vary much when the people in power have a D, as opposed to an R, next to their names. The U.S. involvement in foreign wars doesn't change much when there's a new president or Congress. Taxes and regulations on corporations, as well as CEO salaries, aren't exactly flipping back and forth depending on how cool the man in the Oval Office is.

So then why is it even a factor for liberals? Actual evidence is not even considered. Just like Americans love the coolness of celebrities and athletes, so too do they seek that quality in politicians. And when most celebrities profess liberal positions (see earlier chapter), that only makes their side seem cooler.

Nobody seems hip by saying they're Republican. Maybe a little bit by claiming to be libertarian, but still not much. But liberals could make much better choices if they graduated from their high-school outlook on life and started looking at things that truly do matter.

They Hate Conservatives

"If there is true evil in the world, it is Republican conservatives." — Moby, musician

Aside from the dorky stereotype of the Republican as discussed in the previous chapter, there are many other stereotypes of those on the right, some of which are true, but which nonetheless are certainly poor reasons for considering yourself a liberal.

Perhaps the biggest misconception is that that anyone with a conservative viewpoint is automatically part of the "Religious Right." Those with this misconception think that if you want to lower taxes, for instance, you must also believe that abortion should be illegal even in cases of rape or incest. (Not necessarily knocking people who think that, but it is not a popular opinion.) In fact, some surveys show at least half of those who consider themselves Republicans "supported" Roe vs. Wade.

The truth is that the so-called "Religious Right" are only a small part of American conservatives. In fact, most surveys of registered Republicans have found that not even a majority are very religious. Furthermore, the number of religious white conservatives is on the decline. But many liberals just see the portrayals of former presidential candidate Rick Santorum or the late Jerry Falwell, for instance, on MSNBC or Huffington Post and assume that anyone who thinks that a certain EPA regulation does more harm than good must also be for gay conversion therapy.

It's time for liberals to understand that not everyone who disagrees with them on certain issues fits their incorrect stereotype of what a conservative is.

They Don't Want You Touching Their Handouts

"Food stamps are an investment in our future." —Donna Brazile, former Democratic campaign manager

Many progressives are that way because they receive things from the government that they don't want to stop getting. These include Medicare, Medicaid, Social Security, various tax breaks, or welfare.

I've met plenty of senior citizens who would seem like they'd be anything but "liberal" who still vote for Democrats almost religiously. With enough digging, I find out that they fear that Republicans will take their Social Security and Medicare away. Indeed, a few Republicans do *sometimes* discuss restructuring these programs or adjusting retirement ages, but no serious reforms have happened, even when Republicans controlled both houses of Congress and the Presidency.

Medicare and Social Security make up roughly half of our federal government spending. We've now reached the point where over half of American households are receiving some kind of government assistance, and that's just from the federal government. Many, like those getting Social Security, have paid into the system and feel perhaps justifiably that nobody should be reducing the money they get "back." But that means all the people on these huge programs, as well as welfare, Obamacare subsidies, etc. will continue to vote for the candidates who promise not to touch or expand these programs.

Benjamin Franklin once said, "When the people find that they can vote themselves money that will herald the end of the republic." That is essentially what all these entitlements are. Politicians, both on the left and the right, know that when you rob from Peter to pay Paul, Paul will vote for you and your friends so that you can do it some more!

So what's wrong with that? I've discussed The Big Four earlier, the four big reasons that encapsulate why I believe big government spending programs are terrible. They are immoral, unconstitutional, and ignorant of history and economics.

Clearly, those who vote on the left just because they don't want anybody touching "their" stuff are not thinking things through. Certainly, Republican office holders are for the most part not working to do anything about the problem either, including when it comes to military spending. But using your desire to get money and privilege (oh, the irony) from the government as a reason to consider yourself a liberal and keep voting for Democrats is the epitome of selfishness, shortsightedness, and economic illiteracy.

They Are Part of the "Mob"

"True patriotism isn't cheap. It's about taking on a fair share of the burden of keeping America going." — Robert Reich, former Democratic economic advisor

No, I haven't done any research, anecdotal or otherwise, in the political tendencies of those in the Mafia. I am instead referring to the liberals that have the "mob mentality" – that is, they believe that if they are in favor of something, everybody should be forced to support it. It's the idea that if I personally want people to have X, then everybody must be required to pay for it.

This applies to so many things in modern American society. People want to use the government as a tool to get their favorite charities made mandatory. What is an entitlement program (Medicare, Social Security, Medicaid, Obamacare, etc.) after all but a "charitable endeavor" that is required by law (i.e. the threat of incarceration if you don't comply)?

I like to donate my money to cancer research. That's my choice, because it's something I believe in and wish to spend my own personal money toward. Can you imagine if I thought that everyone should be *forced* to give some of their money to that particular cancer research? Great, you say? Okay, but I also donate to ten other charities. Now I want to force you to give your money to those charities, too. No, I'm not posting something on social media where I *encourage* my friends to support these particular causes. In that case, people that want to support me, or willingly decide that they want to donate an amount of their choosing to that particular target do so. No, instead I'm trying to get my congressperson to vote for a bill that funds these particular causes. In other words, because I like something, you must pay for it. It's a mob mentality. You can see how this would never end.

And that's exactly what has happened. We have tons of what are essentially charitable causes, in theory anyway, that are not optional because at some point liberals (and sometimes Republicans who wrongly identify as conservative) said the American people need to "fund" X. So we have the aforementioned government-mandated "charities," and those are just the ones with which we're most familiar.

Not only do we now get locked up in a prison cell if we don't pay for these causes, but it means less money goes to actual private charities where government inefficiency is absent, and where we get to decide how our money is spent. Wait, you say. Haven't I seen the reports of how little of their revenue some of these *private* charities actually direct toward the cause they claim to aid? Yes, there are some that have such "inefficiencies." But that's no problem. Don't give them your money! That's the beauty of voluntary charity. You choose who you think will best utilize your hard-earned money. You decide who controls it and where it goes. If it was spent poorly or didn't have the desired effect, you stop giving to that charity. With the mob mentality, your choice is gone. You don't get to decide which of the charities that provide medical aid to senior citizens, for instance, your salary will go to. You don't get to *not* contribute to Medicare because it's so grossly mismanaged. The decision has been made for you.

Government force and monopoly have crowded out much of the voluntary aspects of society. There aren't a ton of options for those of us who wish to donate money to help pay for medical care for senior citizens. Most people just assume the government is already "taking care" of it and taking taxpayer money in the process, so no one thinks of starting or donating to such an organization.

But it doesn't end with domestic entitlement programs. Sometimes people are upset about tragedies that occur in other countries. So rather than voluntarily sending my money to aid the people of Darfur, let's say, I'm going to try and force everyone to cough up their earnings to aid in this cause. It's important to me, so therefore it better be important to you. You don't get any say in how it's spent, if it just goes to the local warlords instead, or if supplies that are purchased are bought for a good deal, for instance. But if you don't pay it, time to put you in a cage.

The mob mentality also applies to paying taxes, believe it or not. You hear about celebrities and the Warren Buffets of the world that say we should all "pay our fair share" or that they wouldn't mind paying more in taxes. Did you know that you can give extra money to the IRS or the Department of the Treasury? You just go to their webpage and they'll take your voluntary contribution! But no, that's not what leftist wealthy people meant. They meant they want us to all be forced to pay more in taxes, and *then* they'll give more. So it's not just that they are willing to. They'll only do it if we all have to.

Of course, lefties who haven't done actual research beyond a *Washington Post* article here and there are afraid: If we don't force people to pay for all these things, what would happen to those that need help? Surely you're not suggesting that people would just donate the money they saved from reduced taxes to help everyone get healthcare, food, and shelter, right?

Actually, I am saying just that. No, not everyone in our country is super generous, and there are plenty of people that would keep their money for themselves. But even a cursory look at history before the massive entitlement/welfare state we find ourselves in reveals that people in the U.S. (and other countries) took care of each other far more effectively and responsibly than they are forced to via Uncle Sam today. Through something called "mutual aid societies," people came together to support each other as needed. There was no rampant abuse in the system, like "welfare queens" or people on disability that were perfectly able to work. The organization's members quickly would realize when fraud was occurring and be able to deal with it. Through voluntary actions and keeping these charities more or less local, those who needed help were given it. The great fear of people dying on the streets without the government forcing us to be nice to our fellow citizens is simply not reality.

Then of course, there are the mob-mentality liberals that bemoan perceived problems with things we consume. It's so terrible, they say, that there are all these harmful chemicals in makeup, or whatever other consumer product just made its rounds on social media. Oh, and it's so awful that there are all these trans fats or GMOs in certain foods. Most obvious solution – don't buy them! Let people who still want them, spend their money on them. But no, we need to take action. We're going to all be forced to live under new rules because of the mob mentality. Let's get laws passed that either ban these things or that require certain labels or testing on these products. Maybe even a higher tax on certain products that contain them!

But besides being immoral to dictate to producers how to run their businesses, the law of unintended consequences is clear. What happens? Products become more expensive. Some companies even go out of business because of the expensive and onerous new regulations. People lose their jobs and entrepreneurs may see their life savings wiped out. People who thought of entering the field with new ideas suddenly realize the red tape is too cumbersome, and innovation doesn't occur because of all these barriers to entry, as economists call them.

Can't we just let people be responsible for their own bodies? Can't we expect grown adults to decide on their own what they wish to consume? Shouldn't we take some personal responsibility and be more cautious when we smear some product on our eyelids or swallow some herbal supplement? No, liberals wish to treat us all like children, depending on Mother Government to tell us what is okay and what isn't. It's because the left wants us to all have to live by the same standards, whether we all want to or not.

Progressives should do some serious reading to realize that one of the major facets of their political belief system is predicated on a simple misunderstanding, and an immoral desire to force their subsequently concocted beliefs on everyone else at the point of a gun.

They Seek a Utopia

"You've got to pay something back so that everyone can have a chance. A 2% tax on the wealthiest fortunes can let us provide universal Pre-K, universal free college, cancel student loan debt for 95% of Americans—and still have a trillion dollars left over." — Elizabeth Warren, (D-MA), United States Senate

Wouldn't we all love to live in a perfect world? A world where war, poverty, disease, prejudice, inequality, injustice, environmental problems, and violence didn't exist would be wonderful. The problem is that it's a fantasy. We can work toward these goals the best we can, and certainly everybody would in some way like to achieve them, but some liberals are so committed to this utopia that they've lost sight of reality.

One of the big problems progressives have is their misunderstanding of the word "should." They say everyone *should* have excellent health care, workers *should* have higher wages, and many even say college *should* be free. Whenever a liberal says something *should* exist, what's missing is the *how*. Either there isn't an answer to that question, or it's just assumed that we will be forced to pay for the given *should*, even if history and economics show that our confiscated money doesn't turn into positive results and only makes things worse. What non-liberals realize is that there's a difference between what *should* be, and what government intervention actually accomplishes. Liberals' idea is that if only we passed the right laws or elected the right people with the right knowledge and the right experience, we could fix all the problems of the world. Instead liberals *should* discover the meaning of the term "unintended consequences."

The Big Four discussed earlier tells us that all these plans for utopia should be scrapped. They're immoral, unconstitutional, ignorant of history, and foolishly uneconomical. I applaud the ambition that some liberals possess when they seek to perfect the world. But the naivete is laughable. Or, rather, it would be if their wishes didn't lead to such devastating and destructive results. Liberals need to look at reality instead.

They Are Shortsighted Thinkers

"But we have to pass the bill so you can find out what is in it." — Nancy Pelosi (D-CA), United States House of Representatives

A lot of what liberals believe really does make sense, albeit only on the surface. Their thinking tends to be very shortsighted. We know they don't look at history or economics, but it turns out that they don't even look at actual data. They find themselves making decisions based on all too simple and undeveloped thinking.

Let's take welfare. If poor people exist, and we know it's nice to help people that are less fortunate, let's make sure we all help them. Tax everybody and give that money to poor people. Makes sense. But that overly simplistic premise has led to all the problems we currently find ourselves in – a government that spends more than it takes in, an economy that is far more stagnant than it could be, people out of work, single mothers with more kids than they can afford, entitlement programs that are unsustainable for future recipients, less money available for actual opportunities to employ people at higher rates, a decline in entrepreneurship and innovation, and so on and so on. That's not even touching upon the Big Four expressed earlier about why these government programs shouldn't exist in the first place.

Let's tackle another one. People should get paid more money. Let's increase the minimum wage. That will make those people who don't earn a lot get more money. Simple. Except it doesn't work that way. Again, unintended consequences appear. Companies can't just magically afford to pay this increased money and all the government requirements that come with it (like payroll taxes, for example). So what happens? Jobs get cut and the very people liberals were trying to help end up getting hurt as they are now without employment and struggling to find it. Poverty doesn't decrease. Jobs for the poor do. Most of those who do see any benefits from increased minimum wage don't even live in poor households, believe it or not! They don't fit the profile of that single mother struggling to make ends meet to support her kids.

Let's take another example of shortsighted thinking. Medical care is expensive. Never mind why it got that way. (We'll discuss later). Liberal solution? Make it "free"! Okay, sure, that really just means other people have to pay for it. Making it free is just intuitive thinking though. But the reality is not so simple. Despite what we hear from politicians, media outlets, and college professors, there are some terrible consequences of not only "universal" or "single payer" health care, but also of any government-funded and government-regulated health care program, like Medicare and Medicaid. By getting the government involved at that level, a lot of things happen. Costs actually go up, and drug prices and medical procedures become more expensive, although it may not seem like that to those who don't pay directly for it, or even those who do through taxes. Companies go out of business. Demand increases. Wait times get longer and personal choice of what procedure you'd like done are less and less your choice. Innovation decreases because there's less of an incentive for companies to do so when they're hampered by government regulation and have less potential for profit. The quality and availability of medical care decreases. It's happened throughout the world and is already happening here.

But finding out that these ideas that seem so intuitive are actually fundamentally flawed requires work. You can't find this stuff out just by chatting with likewise shortsighted-thinking family at Thanksgiving. It requires actual research, which is often hard to find unless you know what to look for. It's not going to appear on your social media feed or in the top of your Google search. Liberals need to step beyond what seems like "common sense" and realize that the real world is more complicated. They need to look at the bigger picture.

They Seek Payback

"There was a time not too long ago when American seniors were too often forced to go without food, medicine, and quality healthcare. But thanks to transformative programs like Social Security, most seniors in this country are provided the opportunity to live with the stability and peace of mind they have earned and deserve." — Mike Quigley (D-IL), United States House of Representatives

Some liberals simply believe that the world owes them something. Whether it's people who belong to an ethnic minority group, people who've simply worked hard and haven't achieved much financial success, or those who have paid a huge portion of their earnings into the government's coffers (who hasn't?), many people identify as liberals because that's the group that pushes for society (government) to give them what they feel they deserve.

Ethnic minorities have been treated pretty horribly in this country. African-Americans have been enslaved and then later subjected to racist practices, predominantly by federal, state, and local governments. Native Americans, or American Indians, also received terrible treatment during the early part of European settlement of the Americas and continued to be treated poorly as the United States expanded westward. (Despite what our government school textbooks tell us, members of Native American tribes at the times weren't always just innocent victims. But plenty of times, they were.) Hispanic Americans, particularly those of Mexican descent, have faced discrimination, as have Jewish Americans, Japanese Americans, Chinese Americans, and the list goes on. (As mentioned in an earlier chapter, we won't include Irish Americans and Italian Americans, because apparently if your skin is light enough, it's okay to make jokes at your expense and past discrimination is often forgotten. This probably also explains the acceptable use of humor to put down Russians and Canadians, as well.) Sometimes, members of these groups seek some sort of reimbursement, whether literally some form of financial reparation, special treatment, Affirmative Action, or just some intangible idea of payback. Who better to give this to them than politicians from the Democratic Party, who often preach the ideas of helping the downtrodden ethnic minority who supposedly remains the victim of systemic racism?

Then of course there are those that have worked hard all their lives and haven't become Warren Buffet, Elon Musk, or Bill Gates. Rather than realize that envy does not excuse theft, they look to the government to level their outcomes with those of whom they are jealous. They are willing to have working Americans pay even more in Social Security taxes, for instance, to preserve the program for themselves. In fact, many Americans feel the government should make sure that they have food and clothing. Most liberals feel that wealth should be distributed more evenly. How to do that? Take it from the wealthy through taxes. Shame on those rich people for their success (or luck)! We've discussed how this is unconstitutional, immoral, inefficient, and just plain dumb in previous chapters. But it's pretty clear who people with that mindset are most likely to vote for.

They Are Hippies Forever

"The civil rights movement was very important in my house, and then Vietnam was very important 'cause there were two boys, so I came of age during a very heated political climate." — Al Franken (D-MN), former member of the United States Senate

Some liberals are just stuck in the 1960s. Back then, there were some causes truly worth supporting. The 20-year conflict in Vietnam surely might have merited criticism. And while the military had already been ordered to be racially integrated in 1948, and educational segregation at the hands of the government had been ruled unconstitutional in 1954, unfair practices (usually at the hands of the government) were still in place that negatively affected ethnic minorities. In 1964, the Civil Rights Act was signed, which legally ended discrimination and segregation that had been a part of Jim Crow Laws, followed by the Voting Rights

Act in 1965 and the Fair Housing Act in 1968. (Were these acts needed? Or were they just public statements to gain more support by politicians who were following societal trends rather than setting them? This is contested, but we rarely hear any legitimate criticism from mainstream media sources.)

While the 1960s are long gone, the hippie, whether an actual original from that era or some younger individual who has today taken up the cause, is still out there. Yes, war still exists, and there are certainly conflicts the U.S. is involved in that deserve protest, but hippies only seem to be vocal about ending conflicts abroad when a Republican president is in power. In fact, when a Republican president suggests lessening our overseas involvement, liberals often change their tune and attack such a notion, as they did when Donald Trump announced plans to scale down troop commitment in Syria.

The other cause hippies still cling to is the alleged discrimination against ethnic minorities and the state of the poor. Yet when we see how much progress has been made in both of those areas since the '60s, it's hard to imagine how hippies could still be fighting for such a "won" cause. Discrimination certainly still exists, but often it's against whites and Asians instead of the hippie's perceived victims of injustice, African-Americans and Hispanics.

While hippies and other liberals still believe blacks and Hispanics are frequently mistreated because of their skin color or ethnicity by police and the criminal justice system, the actual data doesn't show bias to be the cause. Disparities in criminal justice statistics don't prove that racism is to blame, as mentioned earlier, but looking at complex issues with an eye for nuance is not the way of the hippie (or the liberal in general.) Again, should we be upset that men are far more likely to be shot by police or incarcerated by the justice system than women? Aren't there other possible explanations other than inherent prejudice in the system?

Women, too, as you've read in a previous chapter, don't face the struggles they once did to any serious degree. In fact, we've gone to the other extreme when it comes to previously persecuted groups, where people are afraid to say anything deemed the least bit offensive lest they lose their job, get kicked out of their college, or even have their career ruined.

The modern-day equivalents of hippies are often called "social justice warriors," although they may call themselves "activists." These are the people that are always protesting some perceived atrocity and coming up with new victimized groups on a daily basis, it seems. Rather than celebrate the success of individuals, they lay blame for life's woes mostly on straight white men, and act as representatives for other groups based on ethnicity, class, gender or gender *identity,* or sexual orientation. They are perhaps more dangerous than their hippie predecessors because they attack ideas like free speech and favor things that have led to mass murder and starvation, such as socialism or communism. They frequently can be found shouting over someone with whom they disagree or decrying the evils of capitalism while holding an iPhone in one hand and a Starbucks cup in the other.

Social justice warriors and hippies are stuck in a time warp. They will forever be fighting for a cause that no longer exists and creating a new one if need be. If they would only look at issues of serious import, perhaps they could toss their tie-dyes, sandals, and Che and Bernie t-shirts and start voting for the right people.

They Are "Environmentalists"

*"The entire North polar ice cap may
well be completely gone in five years." —
Former Vice President Al Gore in 2008*

like clean air, clean water, and the idea that it would be nice to preserve as much of the natural world as possible. The idea of deforestation, loss of animal habitat, and pollution are all disturbing to me. I think they are upsetting on some level to most people. I am under the impression that climate change is real, at least in part due to human activity, and I don't want that change to be detrimental to life on earth.

However, some liberals start off with those ideas but take them to extremes. Let's look at pollution. The air and water quality in the United States has been improving, and on a dramatic scale, despite what many believe. This is primarily due to changes in technology, in large part perhaps because of the regulations set in place by the government, dating back to the 1960s and 1970s. While as a libertarian I wonder if these goals could have been better achieved without government edict, nonetheless, great progress in air and water quality has been made and it continues to improve.

The left believes that it is the duty of all of us to change how we live, or at least that's what they contend. Many of the celebrities (see the Fantasy Land chapter) that advocate for governmental policies and increased regulations in order to improve the environment, end up not practicing what they preach. They still fly in their private jets (far more costly to the environment than just being a passenger in a mass-transit jet), buy gasoline-consuming cars, and buy large homes that require more electricity (often created by the burning of coal) and use more "non-sustainable" building materials.

The problem is that lefties continue to push for more and more restrictions that hurt everyone else. Government spending skyrockets for subsidies to "green" energy companies because otherwise many consumers wouldn't spend their own money voluntarily on products that are less reliable, less efficient, and not proven to make any real dent in overall environmental health. People have their private property seized or have onerous restrictions placed on what they can do with that property if an organism protected by the Endangered Species Act is found on it. Fracking, propelled by capitalism, not the government, is frowned upon, even though it has led to finding huge energy reserves that in turn were able to help the U.S. gain some energy independence and reduce greenhouse emissions at the same time. Furthermore, the truth is that there is no evidence it harms drinking water, despite everything we've been told by the left. They said that the unsafe levels of lead found in tap water in Flint, Michigan were due to fracking and government not doing enough to keep people safe. It turns out, neither was true. The "crisis," factfinders discovered, was the result of government's overreach, not inaction.

I am not a climate change "denier." I also think that label is so demeaning, and the discussion around this phenomenon often verges into decidedly unscientific hysteria. Climate change has always happened, and it continues to do so. The globe at various points has been warming, and some of those times the change was probably at least in part caused by human activity. However, it is highly unlikely that the impact of increased warming will be anything like the disaster scenarios that liberal environmentalists put forward. The idea that it's been the cause of a worsening in the severity of hurricanes is a theory that is certainly not backed by the evidence. Nobody likes the idea of polar ice caps melting, or seeing skinny polar bears, but the ice level has always varied. The horror stories are full of hyperbole with dire predictions that were already supposed to have come true that simply never did.

But even given the actual harm the planet has and continues to suffer, the solutions put forth by liberals are ridiculously expensive, unrealistic, and have huge impacts on the costs of living for a large number of people. The Green New Deal that was promoted by members of Congress in 2019 and continues to be pushed under different names had completely unrealistic ideals for nationwide renewable energy, depending on windmill farms on some mythical span of land so large that it didn't exist. But even if all that were possible, and all the costs in terms of all the other aspects of our lives were "worth it to save the planet," Green New Deal proposals and others like it are unlikely to have any significant impact on global temperatures, even if everyone participated the way the proposed laws and Paris Climate Accords wish.

Perhaps one of the starkest examples of misinformation from liberal environmentalists has to do with plastic drinking straws, now increasingly banned or phased out in states across the country. The idea is that plastic straws add to the Great Pacific Garbage Patch and other accumulations of plastic refuse in the world's oceans and harm sea life. However, the primary "statistic" used to back up these governmental overreaches, including large fines and even jail times for straw ban violators, is bogus. The widely repeated contention that Americans use a whopping 500 million straws each day came from a 9-year-old boy. That figure has been debunked but that hasn't stopped it from spreading. Furthermore, while no one wants to see a sea turtle with a plastic straw stuck through its nose, even a complete ban of plastic straws in the U.S. won't do much to stop that. The majority of plastic waste in the oceans comes from other countries that don't have the sophisticated recycling and waste management systems we have here. In addition, the portion of that plastic waste that consists of drinking straws is tiny. But, like most liberal environmentalist ideas, everyone must change their lives by force even if we get no closer to the original goal.

Liberals should at this point let Americans decide how they wish to contribute to environmental change. The problem is that demanding everyone to live their lives so differently asks for people to give up free choice and causes problems, almost always more than these demands solve. Capitalism has already led to changes in technology and will continue to provide appropriate incentives for meaningful improvements to the environment around us. When the ocean's garbage patches got worse and worse at the hands of third world governments, private industry stepped in to clean it up. When national parks got filthy during a federal government "shutdown," private companies came in to clean it up, knowing that their own businesses depended on it. If people are rioting in the streets because the government has spent us into oblivion, there won't be much to celebrate about having a "greener" planet.

They Follow in Their Parents' Footsteps

"I had intelligent, high-minded, liberal parents who wanted to make sure my values were just like theirs." — Jennifer Grey, actress

Political affiliations are one of those things that often run in families. Sure, the very young still tend to be more politically liberal than the more mature, and other factors, like ethnicity and social class certainly play a part, as discussed earlier. But a lot of times, people just automatically follow in their parents' footsteps. Doing so, whether you're conservative, liberal, socialist, or libertarian means you haven't really given much thought to your beliefs. They're sort of just ingrained.

Of course, some research shows that kids that were inundated with those staunch political beliefs will grow up to rebel. So those of you who took your nine-year-old daughter to marches where screaming women wore knit caps meant to resemble their genitalia and screamed at Donald Trump for being a fascist might someday regret that tactic. She might just become a Republican.

Nonetheless, some liberals are just aligning politically the way their parents did. Think about it. Is your political affiliation or set of viewpoints more or less the same as that of your parents? You might be thinking, well, no, I disagree with my parents on a lot of things. But if you generally vote for the Republican candidate, there's a decent chance your parents probably did, too, and the same with those of you who vote for Democrats. Granted, there are plenty of exceptions, but overall, we tend to fall along similar party lines as our parents.

Now think how wrong that is. Basically, it's as though your political affiliation is chosen for you. You likely haven't decided to explore all options fully, and you've just sort of stewed involuntarily in the political upbringing your folks cooked up for you. Conservatives and liberals both do this, but it certainly explains a lot of why people vote the way they do. If liberals would stop and think, "Wait, what if my parents were wrong?" occasionally, maybe they could start making their electoral decisions based on something that really matters.

They've Never Run a Business

"If you've got a business — you didn't build that. Somebody else made that happen." — Barack Obama, 44th President of the United States of America

Some liberals have never been the head of their own company. They've always had a boss and earned a paycheck, but never had everything on the line like someone who runs their own business does. They've never experienced the highs and lows of coming up with an idea and risking their own hard-earned money to see it through. They've also never experienced the slap in the face when the President of the United States tells them it's the government that deserves the credit for their success, not them, as Barack Obama did when he said the quote above.

Had liberals had that experience (only about 10% of workers own a business, but over half of American workers are employed by a small business), they'd likely have a completely different perspective on the proper role of government. Had they ever started and run a business, they'd know that regulations ranging from industry-specific standards that are so numerous they're impossible to follow, to Americans With Disabilities Act impositions that require ridiculous inspections and lead to frivolous lawsuits for having a sink an inch too high, make the challenge of delivering a service or good to those that want it all the more the difficult. Had they ever run a business, they'd know that worker-focused government rules like increased minimum wages, payroll taxes, employer-provided health care, and excessive anti-discrimination legislation cause company owners to hire *fewer* employees, and shy *away* from those with handicaps who could potentially mean big legal liabilities.

We hear about "small businesses" all the time, but sometimes fail to realize just what a huge portion of our economy they make up. When Americans go through the experience of running their own business, it changes them. They begin to understand on a microeconomic level how government policies actually make everyone worse off. It's an experience liberals should go through, too. Maybe they'd rethink their alliances.

They Are Anti-Gun

"We have federal regulations and state laws that prohibit hunting ducks with more than three rounds. And yet it's legal to hunt humans with 15-round, 30-round, even 150-round magazines." — Dianne Feinstein (CA-D), United States Senate, who apparently believes hunting humans is legal

Some people are liberals because they strongly believe in gun control or even banning guns altogether. When shootings happen in schools, nightclubs, and other locations we assumed were safe, while statistically rare but still too frequent, our natural instinct is to say guns are the problem. It's easy to fire a gun, especially a semi-automatic or automatic, much harder than say, stabbing with a knife or strangling. Then when you look at the seemingly high numbers of murders or other violent acts involving guns in the US, coupled with what liberals call a disturbing "gun culture" in this country, it only seems to make sense to say we need to have stronger laws against owning some or any guns.

However, there is so much more that lefties seem to not understand. If a liberal were to avoid gut reactions, and refrain from repeating misleading or downright untrue statements they heard from friends on social media or the nightly news, perhaps they could look beyond their instant shock and disgust at the senseless killings of innocent people. Perhaps they would see the clear patterns that have evolved in U.S. cities and states – a reverse correlation between the number of guns a population has, and the gun violence in that place. Perhaps they'd see that, as one particularly fascinating book's title says, having more guns equals less crime. Perhaps they'd see that when innocent, law-abiding citizens are allowed to have weapons, they are allowed to defend themselves. When they aren't, the evil nutcases out there know that they can shoot at fish in a barrel. This is exactly what happens in so-called "gun-free zones" like schools. Perhaps progressives with all the information would see that the often touted positive results in places in Europe and Australia actually hide troubling realities, such as new black markets in guns, increased murder rates just using other weapons like knives (or cars!) or the fact that mass shootings actually do happen overseas, but just aren't publicized the way they are here. Perhaps they'd realize that minorities and the poor in inner cities are only alive because the gangs that rule their streets know that these otherwise hapless victims might be armed. Or that women who would otherwise be victimized by biologically stronger men have leveled the playing field (when the government doesn't get in their way) by packing heat. Perhaps they'd realize too that we already have many regulations in place which have had little to no recognizable impact on gun violence. Perhaps they'd realize that some of the strongest advocates for "common sense gun control," like celebrities and politicians, have their own armed security guards, luxuries the rest of us can't afford. Maybe they'd learn that many acts of violence, including mass shootings, have been prevented or ended quickly because there was a "good guy with a gun" on hand. Maybe they'd realize at least that "automatic" weapons are already illegal in the United States, outside of the military.

But even ignoring all that data, as anti-gun crusaders do, even if you say we should regulate firearm possession or manufacture more strictly than it already is, or ban handguns altogether, how exactly do you do that? Do we go door to door and into every single home in the United States? Do we violate fourth amendment rights and just begin searching every room? Do we then go into every single car in the United States, searching for weapons there, too? Or do we take the idea of voluntary gun "buybacks" nationwide, collecting weapons from everyone, and just hope that all the bad guys turn them in too?

No, liberals haven't done the actual research beyond a few numbers that seem to make them feel happy. And so they figure that any person who believes that innocent people should not be mowed down in a hail of gunfire must therefore vote for the Democrat. If our safety were so easy to acquire, I wouldn't have bothered writing this book.

They Are Slaves to Peer Pressure

"Pick the target, freeze it, personalize it, and polarize it. Cut off the support network and isolate the target from sympathy. Go after people and not institutions; people hurt faster than institutions. (This is cruel, but very effective. Direct, personalized criticism and ridicule works.)" — Saul Alinsky, "community organizer" and author

Let's face it. Between Republicans and Democrats, or conservatives and liberals, the ones that are typically the loudest are the latter, the liberals. Whether it's on college campuses, during street protests, on social media, or even in family conversations, the ones that get angry and emotional and have no qualms about sharing their political opinions at any time are predominantly on the left. Say what you will about conservatives and Donald Trump, but if the year were

2022 and you went to a Trump speech and then a protest against the overturning of Roe v. Wade, the second one's going to have a lot more blaring drums, hyperbole, violent rhetoric, shouting, and angry eruptions.

When we're surrounded by no-holds-barred outbursts by friends, family, and strangers, it's only natural that many of us will bend with the wind. We want to do what seems popular. We can be followers. It's the same reason when someone starts a dumb trend on Facebook that includes a "challenge" for anyone reading it to do the same, other people amazingly pick up the torch. As though it requires too much personal strength to just say, "Wait, why would I post the color of my underwear?" or "Why would I chime in and say 'me too?'" or "Why would I post a black square just because everyone else is doing so?"

The world is full of followers when it comes to fashion, food, technology, and unfortunately, thought. Yelling about one cause or another, regardless of realities, is just one more low-hanging fruit for the followers in society to latch onto. It would do liberals a world of good if they would start thinking for themselves, and not give into the idea that they have to "fit in" politically.

They Feel Guilty

*"I'm sorry I was born white and privileged.
It disgusts me. And I feel so much
shame." — Rosanna Arquette, actress*

There are a lot of people in our country that feel they are to blame for society's ills. They are usually white and have had some level of "privilege" in their life, whether it includes going to college (perhaps partially or completely paid for by their parents), growing up in a two-parent home, or even owning a car. These Americans may also be inundated with ideas about the past misfortunes of ethnic minorities in our country (yet may not know that those troubles were often at the hands of the government, not always its citizens) or the current perceived misfortunes of ethnic minorities.

They hear things about "white privilege," and that only makes them feel guiltier still. They think how unfair it is that they have the life they have while there are so many poor victims out in society that have only racism and bad luck to blame for their problems. After all, being white means that you automatically have an easy life, right? You get any job you want, never get turned down for a loan, have no problem getting into show business, and if the police pull you over, you're treated to high fives and pats on the back.

If liberals would realize that they shouldn't feel guilty about success or even luck, they could focus on efforts that actually would help the people they claim to support. Unless you personally caused harm to another individual, then you are not to blame of course. Just having a certain skin color or ethnic background does not mean that life was handed to you, or that even if it was, that you somehow owe everyone else.

They're Immigrants Who Never Learned About Our History

"I want to go to Washington to make sure we really have an opportunity to expand health care for folks so that it is accessible to them." — Ilhan Omar (D-MN), United States House of Representatives, who apparently never learned about the Constitution's limits on the role of the federal government

There are many immigrants to the United States who understand the history and background of this country. They know that the Constitution was designed not to create imaginary rights like health care and education (true rights don't come at a cost to other people, after all), but to ensure that the federal government didn't impinge upon our *natural* rights of life, liberty, and property. These same immigrants know that America, for a long time, was about freedom from the tyrannies of governments around the world. It was the place to create the quintessential American dream through determination and hard work, not handouts or excuses. It was a place not to forget the traditions and cultures of one's home country, but to adapt to and embrace new ones.

But not all immigrants understand this background or the vision of America in the context and time of its founding. Yes, they can pass a basic citizenship test that many native-born Americans couldn't. But beyond that, they may expect America to give them all the benefits of a more socialized government that other countries, perhaps even their home countries, give. They may think of America as just like any other modern, Western nation, except with more ethnic diversity, and not enough socialism. They may wish America would just embrace single-payer health care, as if it were somehow "behind the times." They may say things like, "Well, back in England" or, "Well, in Mexico…" making one wonder why they ever came to a new country in the first place if they were so happy with things back home. They may try and create an America in the image of some other place, not understanding that America is not *supposed* to be just like every other place. It's supposed to be the land of liberty, not just Canada South.

The things that these misguided immigrants seek are all parts of the Democratic Party's platform. Therefore, these uninformed immigrants are not just confused; they are liberals. If only they would crack open a book or two with a focus on actual American history, perhaps they could be a better contribution to society.

They're Teachers

"Hillary Clinton is a tested leader who shares our values, is supported by our members, and is prepared for a tough fight on behalf of students, families and communities. That fight defines her campaign and her career." — Randi Weingarten, President of the American Federation of Teachers

Some liberals are public school teachers. (You may recall that I am, too.) Why are they liberal? As with all government employees, public school teachers' salaries, benefits, and work requirements are determined by voters, their elected representatives, or government bureaucrats. They naturally want work conditions that they feel are more advantageous, and they perceive Democrats as the elected officials that are more likely to give them what you want. The Dems are often not concerned with the interests of taxpayers, so they are more likely to give public school teachers the financial incentives they desire in exchange for their vote and for them obtaining the perception of being a "supporter of education."

Republicans are perceived to be more often in favor of the wealthy, not those poor kids in inner cities who need things like smaller class sizes, technology and other resources. Plus, Republicans don't understand, as Democrats do, that teachers will be of higher quality if they are well-paid and have generous health care and pensions. So go the liberal teacher talking points anyway.

During the Los Angeles teacher strike in 2019, I went against my own conscience and struck. Why? Because I knew if I didn't, I would be shunned by my fellow teachers and even some of the parents of students for years to come. I felt cowardly that I hid my feelings inside, but I feared the backlash would make coming to work every day in the future a source of discomfort.

It's not that I didn't want some of the things that the union was demanding. Who doesn't want a 6.5% pay increase? Other issues were also ones that come up all the time: smaller class sizes, and more support staff like counselors and nurses. Sure, as a teacher, I would like those things, too. But I didn't and don't like the idea of walking out of your job because you don't get what you want. We're not living in the days of unsafe working conditions in a factory, for one thing. The teachers simply wanted some stuff, weren't getting it, and decided that they would just not show up to work to compel the district to give them what they wanted.

I had a real problem with that sort of forceful, childish approach. Because of longstanding agreements and state laws, our employer, the Los Angeles Unified School District, could not fire us for not showing up to work. They could hire substitute teachers temporarily, but most substitute teachers were intimidated by angry teachers who would hiss, boo, demean, and even spit at anyone crossing a picket line. Those substitute teachers also knew that if they were a "scab" they would never be hired in the future to fill in when one of those striking teachers called in sick.

Imagine if you started a business and one day your employees decided that they wanted more money or different working conditions. You explained that you couldn't meet all their demands as you simply did not have enough money to afford all of them. So they decided to not work, to march outside your business with picket signs, and to repeat simplistic chants about being "united." Of course, you're not going to let some group manipulate you into doing something you can't do! So you fire them and find someone that is willing to do the job for the benefits you offer. Well, the school district isn't allowed to do that. Essentially, the teacher's union has all the power and can hold an entire city's population of school children's feet to the fire.

In defense of teachers, one might say they also aren't living in an entirely analogous situation to the one described above. In the business situation, if your employees weren't happy, they could try and find a job elsewhere where they could find a higher perceived value for their labor, but the school district in a big city essentially has a monopoly on teacher jobs. There are certainly private schools (most pay a much lower salary than their public school counterparts), or other smaller districts, in this case in incorporated cities like Beverly Hills, Compton, or Burbank. But again, those pickings are slim, and are not likely to have better offerings, at least in terms of salary.

Fortunately, there are charter schools where teachers could apply to try and get a situation where some of their demands are met. Here's the irony: Part of the platform of the Los Angeles teachers' union, as well as unions across the country, was to reduce the number of charter schools!

Charters were (and continue to be) vilified by teachers at traditional public schools. Signs at the marches I attended decried the "privatization" and "dismantling" of public education. Speeches attacked "corporate greed" at the hands of billionaires, assuming that rich philanthropists (like the district's then superintendent Austin Beutner or businessman Eli Broad) who supported the expansion of charter schools must only be in it for the money. It was unfathomable that they just had a different vision of how to improve educational opportunities for students, many of whom were in underperforming schools and had no choice but to attend their local "public school."

Charter schools *are* public schools. The main difference is that they are funded in most cases directly by the state government, rather than through the bureaucracy of the local school district. Because of this, they tend to have more autonomy in terms of hiring/firing and curriculum. They are often *run* by private companies, however, as if that's such a bad thing. My fellow teachers criticized this fact, as well as the fact that some charter company CEOs make several hundred thousand dollars a year in salaries. They also criticized these organizations for making a profit at the expense of "public" schools. But who cares if they make a profit if that's where parents want to send their kids? Besides, for-profit charter schools were made illegal in California in 2018! Only non-profit charter schools are allowed there. The same is true in several other states.

Critics also say charter schools don't take in children with special needs. Of course this isn't true at all. While some studies show that charter schools have fewer children *identified* with special needs than do traditional public schools, that doesn't mean they're not allowing them in! Isn't it possible that parents with children with special needs want all the extra (and often unnecessary) supports their traditional public school provides and don't want them in a charter school where expectations may be higher and excuses lower?

Besides, teachers in "traditional" public schools are always complaining, rightfully in my opinion, about kids that are all too easily labeled "special ed." Kids seem to get away with having poor behavior or receive ridiculous, unfair modifications and accommodations put in place to somehow make them have the "least restrictive environment." Many teachers hate when students who seem to require constant one-on-one attention from their classroom teacher (not just a paraprofessional) are put in their classroom. That one student's "rights" seem to trump the educational rights of all the *other* children who also need their teacher's attention. These teachers may not admit it openly, but they'd love to be in a school where this no longer happened. But tell them maybe a charter with a different approach is the answer and you'll quickly have made an enemy.

However, being at a charter school doesn't always mean higher teacher salaries. Charters often don't have to abide by the incredibly protective laws in place that make it highly difficult to get rid of an underperforming teacher. No, a charter truly does put the student first, not the teacher, in this regard.

Charters have had mixed results, certainly. Students at some charters across the country do the same or worse as their traditional public school counterparts, but many do better. Some charters have made the news for having scandals or inappropriate use of funds. The teachers in unions love to point these things out, as do the media. But what they don't point out is that the alternative is often a school that has teachers who know they can't get fired, and a top-down, bureaucratic curricular approach where students often underperform. With a charter school, at least parents have a choice. They are no longer stuck with whatever school they happen to live nearby. In Los Angeles, the vast majority of students in charter schools are African-American, Latino, and from low-income families.

No, despite the chants of "fighting for students" and trying to "save public education," the striking teachers wanted to make their own jobs better. They felt that it's not fair that "unregulated" charters got away with too much and that it put the future of their own jobs in jeopardy as more and more parents opted to put their kids in charter schools.

So it's clear that many teachers are not thinking about their students when it comes to politics, but about what they feel they deserve for all their hard work. Even if we excuse those perhaps understandably selfish thoughts, does it now make sense why teachers vote for Democrats?

No! As with many other states with vocal teachers' unions who shout about the same concerns as the ones in Los Angeles, California is a blue state! All of this happened under the watch of elected Democrats. California had a Democrat for governor, a Democrat-controlled legislature, and a Democrat state superintendent of instruction. Even the mayor of Los Angeles was a Democrat. The predominantly left-leaning electorate of Los Angeles voted for a school board which chose a superintendent who supported reforms such as increased acceptance of charter schools. So voting for a full house of Democrats still led to conditions where teachers were unhappy.

Another reason why teachers are usually liberals is because they believe the biggest problem in public schools is a "lack of funding." Time and time again, these advocates say public schools are "underfunded," we spend more money on prisoners than students, and so on and so on. While the latter may be true, the connection between spending and student success is completely misunderstood. In fact, we've seen that spending doesn't correlate with test scores. That's right – states that spend more per student than other states don't necessarily have better results, and vice versa! In addition, as spending from federal and state governments has increased over the years, student test scores have remained stagnant! Clearly, more money is not what's needed. If government-funded schools, whether traditional or charter, are going to succeed, they need to cut spending on bloated bureaucracies, unnecessary positions, and grossly overpriced materials, be able to hire/fire teachers according to performance, and expel/suspend students who make learning difficult for others or who don't put in effort into their work.

But of course, there is more to it than just "fixing" it. Government-run systems are ineffective. You've certainly been to the post office and the DMV. This is what happens when government is in charge of something. Is this really the system our children should be in? Teachers should realize that the problem is not "billionaires" influencing the school board or a rash of "unregulated privatization." The problem is public education period. When the market is thrown to such an unnatural place with the use of huge sums of taxpayer-siphoned funds, we get the growth of enormous bureaucracies and unions which all fight over those funds. The school choice movement is at least a solid compromise toward using those funds competitively in a more market-oriented fashion. While my libertarian wish of ending government's role in education is incredibly unpopular, at least teachers might consider a small step in the right direction – not basing their political allegiances on foolish and unreliable assumptions, and no longer voting for Democrats.

They Blame Capitalism and Free Markets

"Capitalism is against the things that we say we believe in — democracy, freedom of choice, fairness. It's not about any of those things now. It's about protecting the wealthy and legalizing greed." — Michael Moore, documentary filmmaker who has yet to return the millions he's made in ticket, DVD, and streaming sales

Some liberals have a general dislike toward capitalism. They think that capitalism makes the rich richer and the poor poorer. They think our environmental problems are all due to unrestricted free markets. They blame capitalism, in fact, for an endless list of society's ills, from unaffordable health care to homelessness, and some of the biggest economic downturns, such as the Great Depression, the 2008 "housing crisis," and the dramatically rising prices and inflation during President Joe Biden's term in office.

None of these ideas are actually true. First of all, we have a highly regulated market in virtually every sector listed above. These regulations and associated ruling bureaucracies are what are predominantly responsible for the so-called faults of capitalism. No other system in history has lifted more people out of poverty and continues to do so. Yes, it has made rich people richer, but it has also made poor people richer.

The free market is based on people making voluntary choices, trading their goods or services for someone else's. Because of competition, prices go down, while innovation and quality go up. Is McDonald's the best food out there? Of course not. But it's (relatively) cheap and if you are willing to trade more of your labor (i.e. pay more money) for a higher quality, more expensive meal, you have that option.

Our problems are caused when the government gets involved, often colluding with more established, larger businesses to presumably protect the consumer, while really limiting their choices, raising costs, and preventing competition. Monopolies, contrary to what our school history books tell us, don't occur because a company "gets too big." They occur when a company gets special privileges from the government to effectively prevent any other company from competing with them. The truth is that vilified companies in our history books like Standard Oil or its head John D.

Rockefeller, while persecuted by the government, did not actually run monopolies. In a free market, another company can and will come along at some point by undercutting another company's prices or providing a better product or service.

Of course, this isn't intuitive. We tend to believe (and have been taught to believe) that the free market is some sort of wild frontier where people are taken advantage of and the less fortunate are left to starve. Nothing could be further from the truth. If progressives would realize this, perhaps they would get out of the free market's way and make everyone better off.

Most people, conservatives and liberals alike, are so mentally enveloped in the ways of our government-regulated economy that they can't even imagine, and often fear a world where government doesn't have its hand in everything. But it's not just a dream of the future. It actually existed in the past and even still thrives in many ways today.

What was life in this country like before Medicare, Medicaid, Social Security, and every one of the myriad welfare or subsidy programs that exist at all levels of government today? Were people starving in the streets or dying of diseases because they couldn't afford to treat them?

The fact is the private sector – AKA regular people – took care of each other, by choice, and far more efficiently than any government program ever could. As discussed in a previous chapter, fraternal organizations called mutual aid societies provided for communities. Roads were even built before and after government took on the task. Schools even existed before government got involved. Parents taught their kids at home or sent them to a local school run by volunteers from the community, often for free or for an affordable fee.

Think about today. Despite tons of regulations on basically everything in our country, we still turn to the private sector for advice on what's best, not some government bureaucracy. United Laboratories makes sure our electrical appliances are safe. To find out if a restaurant or a hotel in a new city is any good, we don't typically go onto the local government's safety website to see what the health inspector has to say. We use things like TripAdvisor. TripAdvisor makes money by delivering accurate reviews, and it puts pressure on restaurants and hotels to improve their quality and service, far better than some edict from City Hall. We also use the Auto Club or Consumer Reports to help us make informed decisions, not an official stamp from some uninformed government bureaucracy.

When we look for any local business, we don't check with the city to see how long the company has been paying business taxes or the state to see if any cases have been filed against it. We look on Google Reviews or Yelp. Again, the private sector regulates itself. If a business which isn't protected by the government fails to satisfy the demand of customers, word gets around and people stop going there. This is far more effective and efficient than constantly using the heavy hand of government to regulate all manner of businesses.

We're taught that capitalism has failed us, leading to the rise of Rockefeller and his oil monopoly, which wasn't true at all. He actually cut prices to remain competitive and was simply the best supplier around for a time. That's happened throughout history. Remember social media platform Myspace? Computer giant IBM? Mega-retailer Sears? They often get their turn in the spotlight until a competitor comes along with something more innovative, more affordable, or more desirable in some other way to customers. Again, the only monopolies that exist are the ones where the government gets involved and protects that business from competitors or gives special privileges and subsidies to that business.

As discussed earlier, our government schools continue to perpetuate myths about capitalism, creating more liberals. The so-called Progressive Era, the period from the 1890s to 1920s where the role of the federal government in the private sector was greatly expanded, actually harmed the economy. The New Deal, President Franklin Delano Roosevelt's series of new government programs and regulations between 1933 and 1936 didn't end the Great Depression but lengthened it and made it worse!

No, capitalism is clearly not the enemy it's often portrayed as, but rather a literal savior of society. We should be trying to bring our country back into its embraces in the purest form we can find, not misidentifying the failures of government intervention as failures of the free market. If only liberals would realize these truths, they could start calling for a reduction in the size and scope of government, which would actually help all the people they claim to support.

They Believe Socialism is the Answer

"When we talk about the word 'socialism,' I think what it really means is just democratic participation in our economic dignity and our economic, social, and racial dignity. It is about direct representation and people actually having power and stake over their economic and social wellness, at the end of the day." — Alexandria Ocasio-Cortez (D-NY), United States House of Representatives, who may be in need of a dictionary

A long with those people that have false conceptions of capitalism, there are plenty of people who think social-ism is the solution. Socialism is usually defined as the collective or governmental ownership and administration of the means of production and distribution of goods. So-called "democratic socialists" advocate for this abolition of capitalism through democratic, as opposed to authoritarian means.

Regardless of the distinction, socialism leads to disaster. As Margaret Thatcher once said, the problem with socialism is that eventually you run out of other people's money.

Let's be clear. While countries that still get labeled "capitalist" may have developed strong social safety nets and tons of government entitlements, things that socialist countries also have, that doesn't mean they have yet gone "full socialist." While I certainly advocate for keeping government as much out of our bedrooms and boardrooms as possible, I do think it's important to understand that we can't mix the two systems up.

True socialism means getting *rid* of capitalism. Big government in an otherwise capitalistic system, while also deplorable, can have terrible effects on the wonders of the free market, but that doesn't mean it's gotten rid of capitalism entirely.

Also of note, conservatives and liberals often incorrectly label what we might more correctly call "transferist" ideas as "socialist." Transferism involves using the government to force people to pay for something that you want for yourself or for someone else. Socialism is government control of the means of production.

Wait, the liberal says. Socialism has worked! Look at Scandinavia. Only problem – Scandinavian countries are not socialist (or even as transferist as they once were). While countries like Sweden did tax, spend, and regulate heavily in the past, disaster and even violence ensued, and they started scaling back and embraced market reforms.

What about other parts of Western Europe? Most are not socialist either. Not even "democratic socialist." Those that had elements of socialism in the past are moving away from them because the results were disastrous. We've seen what happened in France, Greece, and Venezuela (actual socialism). Terrible implications for the economy and mass unrest.

So clearly, the countries that are still around that at one time toyed with socialism are only still around and prospering because they moved the other direction before it was too late.

The countries that have had socialism, "democratic" or otherwise, have failed or are in the process of doing so. But members of the Left who favor socialism always say "that wasn't real socialism," "that wasn't democratic socialism," or "that was a corrupt version." Are these advocates of socialism just unaware of the history (and present) that shows it's a disaster, even when it was born in a democratic system? Or do they just think that somehow this time it will be different?

As Thatcher said, socialism runs out of money. Even taxing the rich at an insanely high (and unfair) level won't pay for it. Nearly everybody would have to be taxed more. Fine, you say? It's fine with you to spend most of your days working not for your own money, but for money to go to an inefficient and ineffective, force-utilizing bureaucracy? When you work and don't get paid for it, unless it's a voluntary way of getting the skills needed for your next job, it's not an internship. It might not be slavery, but what would you call it?

And even if you're okay with taking a huge percentage of the fruits of everyone's labor, the results of socialism and socialist practices, "democratic" or not, also create less (if any) innovation in technology, medicine and every other field, lack of choice, and a sharp decrease in the ability to improve your lot in life. Yes, we could make everyone a little more "equal." Equally poor.

Socialism depends on getting rid of the essential incentives to provide a quality good or service at an acceptable price that capitalism has. You've been to the DMV, right? Taken a trip to the post office? You've experienced the long lines and terrible service. You've witnessed the work ethic of employees who know they can't get fired and that any promotions or pay raises they get will be on time served, not on merit. This is government in action, handling relatively simple tasks. You want them exclusively in charge of providing health care? You want them to decide if you really need a medical procedure and when? You want them choosing which professional you can see and what your acceptable course of treatment is? You want to wait months or years for a surgery or procedure, as they do in Canada and the United Kingdom?

No, "free" health care is not free. Call it "single payer," "universal," "Medicare for all" – the reason it's expensive now is not because of the free market and greedy drug companies and insurance providers. Why wouldn't everything in our country be super expensive because of greed then? Surely greedy people don't only work in medicine. The real reason medical insurance and prescription drugs can be expensive is because we already have so much government "regulation" of medicine in place. It limits how many hospitals can be built, demands insurers provide expensive plans to people who don't need or want them or certain aspects of them, and creates so many more regulations that kill the miracle of the free market. Government subsidies further complicate things by raising health care prices. Drug regulations and overly arduous trial processes keep the medicines we need from being in our hands, and onerous requirements keep them so pricey that we wrongly blame "Big Pharma."

When the coronavirus (COVID-19) left many in panic, it wasn't helped by the fact that we had been relying on government institutions to prepare for and oversee the safeguarding of citizens. Those government organizations and their regulations were standing in the way of effective problem solving. The edicts to maintain "social distancing" in order to "flatten the curve" by keeping people at home and shuttering businesses were not just ham-handed ways of trying to save people's lives. Those intrusions into the private sector were designed to prevent the "system" from being overwhelmed. Why would it be overwhelmed? Government regulations had caused a shortage of resources, hospital beds, and medical professionals.

Liberals who favor socialism may also love the idea of free college. Let's understand why college is so expensive in the first place. Yes, many private and public colleges have fancy buildings and highly paid staff that they wish to pay for or expand. And certainly, a big reason colleges charge so much is not to pay for instruction but to fund their own research. But college is still getting more and more expensive every year. That's primarily due to government subsidies. The more government gives to students to help them attend college, the more those colleges raise prices. If colleges know they can charge more because government is giving so much financial aid, then they will. Just imagine then what happens if college becomes "free" or if student loan debt is "forgiven." The price of college will keep going up, and government (i.e. taxpayers) will keep paying more and more to keep up with it. If the government weren't involved, the colleges would only be able to charge what people would be willing to pay. Plus, if colleges are all taxpayer-funded, what if a college wants to offer something that would cost more? If the government doesn't pay for it, the college must toss that idea aside.

As discussed in previous chapters, it's not just medicine and education that are hurt by intrusive government and intensified by socialism or transferism. Even entitlement programs are! Welfare for the poor and the disabled, all manner of subsidies, Social Security, and of course our existing Medicare and Medicaid programs are elements that could be handled much more efficiently and effectively by the private sector. Again, it comes down to the Big Four when it comes to government overreach.

The answer is not socialism. It's less government. If only liberals who favor socialism and transferism would look at history (and the present) and see what the actual consequences of these pie-in-the-sky ideas are, maybe they'd realize that the tool to improving everyone's lot in life is the one thing they are fighting so strongly against – unleashing the free market.

They Are "Pro-Union" and "Pro-Labor"

"And I believe we should strengthen unions which have formed the bedrock of a strong middle class. It should be easier to bargain collectively. That's not only fair, it makes workers more productive, it strengthens our economy." — Hillary Clinton, former first lady, senator, and secretary of state of the United States

Many progressives continue to choose the Democratic Party's candidates simply because they know that when it comes to decision-making, those candidates will back whatever labor unions support. These liberals believe that all of the gains in U.S. history when it comes to safety, salary, and all sorts of working conditions are all a result solely of unionization.

The reality is that, while working conditions were far worse than they are now in many jobs in the U.S., they got better primarily because of capitalism. As discussed earlier, capitalism allows for competition, which also means employers have to compete for labor. Employers have to offer safer conditions, better pay, shorter workdays, and other benefits to lure employees more easily than companies whose offerings are not as attractive.

Today, when unions get involved, especially in the public sector, they are often fighting not for basic safety in a factory, for instance, but higher pay, benefits, and protections for poor performers. These are things that individual employees should be negotiating with their employers. However, unions forbid such negotiations because that means not everyone gets the same thing. Better workers would get better compensation than those who are not as productive.

So if workers in a union decide to strike because they want better compensation or conditions, that's fine. And if their employer is unwilling to give them what they want, then their employer should also be able to fire them and hire employees who are willing to accept their conditions. However, when public sector employees walk off the job, the law says that they can't be fired. In other words, government workers such as teachers, bus drivers, and police officers can hold taxpayers and benefit receivers, such as students and civilians, hostage to their desires for better pay, for instance. In turn, they get protected jobs that make it difficult to fire them and we get lackluster return for our tax dollars.

What's worse is that unions don't necessarily help the best workers out there. Those workers are stuck without the ability to improve their pay based on merit. Plus, by keeping wages artificially high (higher than the market would naturally pay them in most cases), fewer workers are able to be hired, and thus those that are seeking work can't find it.

Meanwhile, public sector unions push for and get such generous pensions for their members that cities and states go broke. But of course the Democrats know that delivering on these truly unsustainable promises gets them in office. Even with these destructive "achievements," Democrats are also not always in the union's corner, even though liberals believe they are. For instance, despite years of Democrats in power in the federal government, many labor reform laws that unions pushed for never got passed.

We've also seen unionization efforts in the private sector, such as with ridesharing apps, specifically Uber and Lyft. Finally, technology and capitalism gave us this amazing, affordable, and convenient system for getting safely from one place to another without the high cost and poor service of a taxi. Drivers and riders both come out ahead. But some drivers, wanting more money and other benefits, have decided it's just not fair. They've been pushing government to come in and regulate these miracles of capitalism, rather than building their own skills and working hard to get the job that gives them what they want without forcing it down someone's throat. As government gives in, what happens? Consumers have to pay more and more and may even opt not to use the once so affordable and convenient services. Fewer consumers using the service means fewer jobs for drivers that would have eagerly accepted the pay these services were originally providing before pro-labor groups stepped in and got government involved.

If liberals would only realize that their diehard support for unions is not only destructive but immoral, maybe they could start supporting candidates that actually can help workers and employers – by getting out of the way.

They Are Elitist When It Comes to Geography

"The flyover states have become the passed over states. That's why red state voters are so pissed off. They don't hate us, they want to be us. They want to go to the party." — Bill Maher, television host

There's a perception, whether stated or not, amongst many West and East Coast liberals that they are better than those in less "geographically desirable" places. In other words, some think that anyone living between New York and LA is a hillbilly, redneck, hick, racist, religious zealot, or idiot.

Of course, many of these liberals came from one such place, but that doesn't matter. They believe they were the smart ones who got out of the primitive "middle America" section of the country and made it to civilization.

So it follows that these geography-prejudiced progressives believe that voting any direction other than left is a sign that you are one of these ignorant rubes between the coasts. To prove that they are not, they must continue to preach the word of the Democrats and let everyone know they are a coaster, or pretty darn close (Chicago liberals somehow gets a pass.)

It's then easy to continue to dismiss election results or polls not as indicative of the opinions of a large number of fellow Americans, but rather as windows into the backward political underpinnings of the ignorant masses who don't reside near an ocean.

If these liberals would consider tossing their bigotry and not judging people based on where they live (or don't live), maybe they could start to evaluate political ideologies and specific beliefs on their merits and leave some of the tribalism behind.

They Believe the Best Presidents Are the Ones Who Do the Most

"I would put our legislative and foreign policy accomplishments in our first two years against any president — with the possible exceptions of Johnson, FDR, and Lincoln — just in terms of what we've gotten done in modern history. But, you know, but when it comes to the economy, we've got a lot more work to do. And we're gonna keep on at it." — Barack Obama, 44th President of the United States of America

When you see rankings of "the greatest presidents," individuals are inevitably placed higher on the list based on how much they "did" during their time in office. Of course, most of these lists are compiled by those in the media or those in academia, who, as discussed earlier in this book, are clearly biased toward the left. So the "historians" who tell us which presidents we are supposed to like the most are always more likely to rate an FDR or an Obama far higher than say a Calvin Coolidge.

But the reality is that we'd be a lot better off if our presidents had done less. As discussed previously, it's clear that big government is not only immoral, but inefficient and damaging. When a president leads the charge, as FDR did when it came to the New Deal or putting Japanese-Americans in prison camps, the results are catastrophic. And yet while liberals tend to believe Obama was a great president for many reasons, one big reason is that he "accomplished so much." Yes, he worsened the quality, availability, and affordability of health care in the United States, but never mind that.

If liberals would realize that the presidents who resist the temptation to levy the harsh and ineffective hand of the federal government to solve any problem that exists, they could see the value that the less active presidents have, individuals who let America continue to grow without the need to score political points. Anyone can say, "I think people deserve" A or B, but it takes real courage and strength to say, "This is not part of my job description. It will be solved much better and faster if I keep the government leviathan out of it." But people who have the dumb, "What did he accomplish?" mindset will continue to vote for the guy who promises the most, even though the ones that do the most are actually the worst.

They Believe Life is Unfair Due to "Privilege"

"Things like racism are institutionalized. You might not know any bigots. You feel like, 'Well I don't hate black people so I'm not a racist,' but you benefit from racism. Just by the merit, the color of your skin. The opportunities that you have, you're privileged in ways that you might not even realize because you haven't been deprived of certain things." — Dave Chappelle, unprivileged African-American comedian worth 60 million dollars

In an earlier chapter, I discussed the guilt that some liberals feel for having had certain fortune in life, often wrongly attributing it to their skin color. In fact, there are plenty of other lefties who agree that white people automatically have life easier. This notion of "white privilege" is a way of discounting anyone's achievements or success by marking it down to the simple fortune of being born with the "right" skin color. It's also a way to push for policies and social justice warriorship in order to get special benefits for "people of color" (Caucasians' "peachy" is not a color, apparently). When white liberal women felt they also wanted to be part of this special class, the term got shortened from "white privilege" to just plain old "privilege." So liberals elect liberals because they feel special policies and attitudes are necessary to combat "privilege."

Of course, the very idea that white people automatically have life easier is complete nonsense. As one article in the references section points out, the white male suicide rate is far higher than their percentage of the population. If white men have been born with this amazing step up compared to the rest of the population, this simply wouldn't be true. Plus, Asians excel beyond whites in major areas such as school scores and credit scores.

In fact, there are many other factors that play into success in life, beyond issues that really don't matter, such as race. Growing up with good parents, especially two of them, makes a big difference in predicting success.

Being an ethnic minority actually gives many a step up these days, including in admission to colleges. It also works for employment. Many companies would rather place an ethnic minority than a white male simply because it makes the employer look or feel good. Professional sports are filled with ethnic minorities. So is the entertainment industry. Furthermore, what a person of color can get away with when it comes to speech is much greater than what a white person can.

Plenty of white people are in prison, in debt, can't find a job, struggle to make ends meet, face discrimination, were born in poverty, come from abusive homes, have diseases, get shot by police, or don't get picked for an Oscar. It's time to stop whining and blaming, and realize that being human is a struggle, no matter what color you are. If liberals realized this, they could focus on things that really matter.

They Are Against War

*"Through my time in the military and my
deployments, I have recognized the importance
of having a Commander in Chief who will not
only go after those who threaten the safety and
security of the American people, but who will also
exercise good judgment and foresight in stopping
these failed interventionist wars of regime change
that have cost our country so much in human
lives, untold suffering, and trillions of dollars." —
Tulsi Gabbard (D-HI), at the time a member of
the United States House of Representatives, and
who has since left the Democratic party*

Being "anti-war" is not a bad position. The United States
has been in too many wars throughout its history, at
the cost of human lives and "treasure" (AKA taxpayer

money). And yet foreign entanglements continue. The U.S. has troops or special ops forces in countries throughout the world. Being anti-war has long been associated with the hippie movement and the left, more broadly. Many liberals, libertarians, and even conservatives believe some or all of these sites of engagement are completely unnecessary to our own security, or worse, make our own security more precarious by creating future enemies.

That is the viewpoint I hold. But I also can understand the argument that at least some of our intervention in foreign affairs is designed to end problems on foreign soil before they can come to harm us here. The longer these engagements go on, however, the more it seems that they actually do nothing for our own safety.

The problem with voting for Democrats based on the idea that we need to reduce or eliminate both our foreign military presence and other involvement overseas is that Democrats aren't much better than Republicans on this issue. Democrats have been the ones behind initiating or continuing many of our biggest wars. Furthermore, despite the rhetoric, many Democratic politicians and liberal media sources who were vocal and brash when it came to denouncing George W. Bush's military interventions suddenly disappeared when Obama initiated new ones and continued or escalated existing ones. Then when Donald Trump discussed moves to end or deescalate U.S. involvement in Syria, it was Democrats who balked. Similarly, it was both Democrats and establishment Republicans who pushed for U.S. involvement of some form when Russia invaded Ukraine in 2022, while some vocal conservatives warned against it.

Opposing military intervention in foreign countries is a cause worth supporting. But considering yourself a liberal or voting for a progressive politician for the sake of advancing that cause doesn't make sense.

They Support Immigration

"More than any other nation on Earth, America has constantly drawn strength and spirit from wave after wave of immigrants. In each generation, they have proved to be the most restless, the most adventurous, the most innovative, the most industrious of people. Bearing different memories, honoring different heritages, they have strengthened our economy, enriched our culture, renewed our promise of freedom and opportunity for all." — Bill Clinton, 42nd President of the United States of America

mmigration has always been an important part of our country. We've heard the cliché, "Our nation was built by immigrants." And, yes, it's true. Traditionally, immigration was a valued component of our country's fabric. And yet opposition to immigration, or opposition to immigration by certain groups, is not a new phenomenon. A supposed bias against immigrants from Central and South America may appear to some liberals to be part of the modern Republican party's unofficial platform, but look not far into our country's history, and you'll see that plenty of "white" immigrants were also treated negatively by Americans of all stripes, whether they were Eastern European Jews, or immigrants from Italy or Ireland.

Government's restrictions on how many immigrants are allowed in, from where, and with what skills are key components of our country's ongoing immigration debate. But one area that continues to get a lot of attention is illegal immigration. Libertarians like myself are not always in agreement on this issue either. Some believe our borders should be open to all. Some believe there should be certain restrictions. But it seems that liberals always think that they are the ones who are kindest, most open, and most welcoming when it comes to immigration, illegal or otherwise.

But is that true? Big names on the left like Barack Obama, Nancy Pelosi, Bernie Sanders, Bill Clinton, and Chuck Schumer may be very critical of Trump for his actions and words against illegal immigrants before and during his time in office, but they are all on record proclaiming some of the same ideas. Even darlings of the labor movement, like Cesar Chavez, were not only vocal against illegal immigration, but Chavez actually sent union workers to beat them up! Leftist hero, indeed. In 2022, mayors of big American cities like New York and Washington, D.C. made a big to-do about being happy to welcome illegal immigrants, until the governors of Texas and Arizona actually bused them directly to their cities. Then they complained that they couldn't handle them!

While it may be hard to fully agree with any one particular open-border or restricted-border policy promoted by any major politician, it is clear that thinking that liberals are the people on the immigrant's side is absolutely wrong. Perhaps they have come to be vocally pro-immigrant only in recent times when a seemingly "anti-immigrant" Republican was in power, or when they realize that those immigrants might be easily duped into voting for Democratic politicians who promise them the world. However, Democrats' actions speak far louder than their words. Being pro-immigration is not a reason to be a liberal.

They Are Anti-Israel

"Remember [the Palestinian] people are occupied and it's their land... [Jews in Israel should] go home... Poland. Germany. And America and everywhere else." — Helen Thomas, late reporter and longtime member of the White House press corps

The history of the State of Israel is long and complex. The ideological and physical battle between Israel and its enemies is centuries old, existing long before a state of Israel was officially declared in the twentieth century. But many leftists in the U.S., both Jewish and non-Jewish, paint Israel as the aggressor. They accuse its government of everything from ethnic cleansing to running an open-air prison camp. But these liberals don't fully understand the historical context of Israel's actions or the reality of the situation.

To start with, it is certainly possibly that Israel's government has made mistakes which have cost lives. Let's admit that. But the reality is that Israel is a tiny dot of land in the middle of a huge territory that includes predominantly Muslim countries, many of whom have attacked Israel in the past and who continue to wish its inhabitants death because of their religion. Yet this territory, which has been the home to many cultures and religions in the past was finally given to Israel as the result of, primarily, two different wars. Like it or not, this is Israel's territory. Wars throughout history have been the final decider in who gets a piece of land that was otherwise in dispute. It's happened in most countries, in virtually all our continents – when people fight over who land belongs to, a war ends up settling it.

In Israel, Arabs of all religions are given more rights than many of them have in Israel's neighboring countries. They have the right to religious freedom and are not persecuted because of gender or sexuality, as they are in neighboring countries.

As far as areas of Israel that are home to Arabs labeled "Palestinians," leftists often like to call these areas "occupied." Here, the Israeli government has soldiers enforcing various restrictions. Why? Because throughout Israel's history, Muslim Arabs have tried to kill Israel's people through any means possible. Israel's leaders know that other than kicking these Palestinians out of Israel, the only other course of action to ensure Israel's security is to have strong security measures in place.

But the terrorist group Hamas has seized control in these territories. They encourage and sometimes force the Palestinians to initiate conflicts, leading Israel's troops to fight back. Inevitably though, the Palestinians or Hamas soldiers seek shelter or initiate their attacks from civilian areas such as hospitals and schools, hoping that Israel will have to hurt civilians to fight back or defend themselves against these attacks. Then, Hamas-backed Palestinians can (and do) win in the eyes of the members of the international community, who either don't know the truth of what's going on or the historical context or are genuinely antisemitic and just want the Jewish nation to fail or cease to exist.

If liberals truly cared about people, they would condemn the role of Hamas and the initiation of attacks and learn why Israel has set up its "occupied" territory the way it has.

They Think Being Liberal Means Being Kind and Caring

"If by a 'liberal,' they mean someone who looks ahead and not behind, someone who welcomes new ideas without rigid reactions, someone who cares about the welfare of the people — their health, their housing, their schools, their jobs, their civil rights, and their civil liberties — someone who believes that we can break through the stalemate and suspicions that grip us in our policies abroad, if that is what they mean by a 'liberal,' then I'm proud to say that I'm a 'liberal.'" — John F. Kennedy, 35th President of the United States of America

once heard a Broadway theater insider, when asked if he was a Republican or a Democrat, reply, "Well, duh, Democrat. I care about people."

Indeed, that feeling is widespread. The Democrats, liberals contend, are the ones that have compassion for people. This is clear in the fact that they support (government) programs that provide money and services for the poor and the elderly, that they believe health care is a right, that they think illegal immigrants should be welcomed here with open arms, that they contend that corporations are evil and are hurting everybody else, that they bemoan how ethnic minorities are downtrodden and need a leg up, that they believe gays and transgendered people are routinely harassed and discriminated against, that they assert that wealth inequalities are a problem, and that they are certain that the earth needs our help to save it from the bad people, and on and on and on.

In essence, many liberals align themselves as liberals because they think that's just what nice people do. Republicans, and for that matter, anyone else, don't care about other people and are just trying to make their own lives better at the expense of everyone else.

The argument can certainly be made that Republicans want to make things better for themselves, but it can also be made for Democrats. It's not "generosity" to give things to someone if it means you're actually taking them from someone else. But that's what most liberal programs are — taking tax dollars from one group to give to another group.

Or getting government so heavily involved in a sector that it ends up negatively affecting that sector for everyone else, like health care, housing, college admissions and student loans, and affirmative action. That's not kindness! It's the exercise of power. It's the idea that, I've voted for people who will get you imprisoned if you don't support my cause. In the meantime, you must work to pay for it, whether or not you support it, whether or not it works, whether or not it's constitutional, and whether or not its effective, or even worse, destructive.

No, kind and caring means you leave people to live their lives with the least amount of meddling by anyone else. Kind and caring means you help others because you wish to, and you do so with your own time and money or gather time and money from those who volunteer to join your cause. If liberals would realize this simple principle, they might change a lot of their thinking.

They're All Dumb Reasons

Truth be told, the biggest problem this country faces right now is bad parenting. It explains why we have kids that grow up to become criminals, why our "schools" are failing, and most relevant here, why kids grow up to vote for bigger and bigger government. Kids are taught that the government is our benefactor, the entity that makes our safety and comfort possible. Without its involvement in every sector of our lives, people would be starving on the streets, racism and sexism would prevent women, gays, transgenders, and ethnic minorities from getting jobs and being victims of violent attacks, anyone that wasn't born with a silver spoon would be working 15 hours a day in a filthy and unsafe factory, our air and water would be poisonous, evil corporations would dictate every aspect of our lives, and only the rich would have health care and quality education.

But if you simply "do your homework," and look beyond what you have been told by everything from the evening news to the morning paper to the Hollywood movie, you would realize that what most of us take as fact is simply untrue. We shouldn't be voting for a politician who tells us that more government action will solve all these problems. We should be voting for a politician that promises to *undo* the harm caused by a hundred years of growing government. It doesn't matter if that candidate has a D or an R next to her name -- she might in fact not have either one.

If you are a misguided liberal who always ticks the box for the person on the left, it's not too late. You can still vote right.

RECOMMENDED READING

Thomas Sowell
tsowell.com

Walter Williams
walterewilliams.com

Larry Elder
larryelder.com

Andrew Napolitano
judgenap.com

Downsizing Government
downsizinggovernment.org

Libertarianism
libertarianism.org

The Cato Institute
cato.org

The Road to Serfdom by Friedrich Hayek
amazon.com/dp/0255365764

Free to Choose: A Personal Statement by Milton Friedman
amazon.com/dp/0156334607

The Anti-Capitalistic Mentality by Ludvig von Mises
mises.org/library/anti-capitalistic-mentality

Reason Magazine
reason.com

Foundation for Economic Education
fee.org

John Stossel
johnstossel.com

Don't Hurt People and Don't Take Their Stuff:
A Libertarian Manifesto by Matt Kibbe.
amazon.com/dp/0062308270

Economics in One Lesson: The Shortest and Surest
Way to Understand Basic Economics by Henry
Hazlitt. amazon.com/dp/0517548232

Double Standards: The Selective Outrage
of the Left by Larry Elder
amazon.com/dp/B075QNH2NG

REFERENCES BY CHAPTER

Introduction: The Premise

Left or Liberal? PragerU. https://www.youtube.com/watch?v=tlIjMJBSnRE

Dumb Reason #1: They Are Slaves to Emotion

Stossel, John. "Who gives to charity?" Townhall.com. https://townhall.com/columnists/johnstossel/2006/12/06/who-gives-to-charity-n841567

Editors. "Liberals are more emotion-driven than conservatives." Society for Personality and Social Psychology. ScienceDaily. https://www.sciencedaily.com/releases/2014/11/141107091559.htm

Rufo, Christopher. "What NYC Must Learn From Seattle's Homeless Struggle." Manhattan Institute. https://www.manhattan-institute.org/what-nyc-must-learn-from-seattles-homeless-struggle?fbclid=IwAR1bVFvJE_T5YziVtfoLu2wMFjRdxgDC47AQOr BBINrzpXbtf9TtIoon_9Q

Dumb Reason #2: They Are Uninformed

Anderson, William. "The Progressive Era, Part 1: The Myth and the Reality." The Future of Freedom Foundation. https://www.fff.org/explore-freedom/article/progressive-era-part-1-myth-reality/

Bentley, Matt. "Study: Does Google have a political bias?" Can I Rank? http://www.canirank.com/blog/analysis-of-political-bias-in-internet-search-engine-results/

Devine, Patrick. "Fox News's Bret Baier explains 'news' vs. 'opinion' to Trump." Yahoo! Entertainment. https://www.yahoo.com/entertainment/fox-news-brett-baier-explains-news-vs-opinion-to-trump-070353057.html

Dwilson, Stephanie Dube. "Is Chris Wallace a Democrat or a Republican? What Are His Politics?" heavy. https://heavy.com/news/chris-wallace-democrat-republican-politics/

Elder, Larry. "Media Bias: It Absolutely, Positively Influences How We Vote." The Elder Statement. http://www.elderstatement.com/2014/04/the-elder-statement-media-bias-it.html

Elder, Larry. "The Truth About the Central Park Five." The Larry Elder Show. https://youtu.be/hwRQztpF6qU

Foley, Ryan. "Conservatives angered by Fox News profile on trans-identified child: 'Horrifying, evil and sick.'" *The Christian Post.*
https://www.christianpost.com/news/conservatives-angered-by-fox-news-profile-on-trans-child.html

Gabbatt, Adam. "Trump v Fox News: why the president is furious at the conservative network." *The Guardian.*
https://www.theguardian.com/us-news/2020/apr/29/fox-news-trump-democratic-talking-points

Kurtzleben, Danielle. "Study: News Coverage Of Trump More Negative Than For Other Presidents." NPR.
https://www.npr.org/2017/10/02/555092743/study-news-coverage-of-trump-more-negative-than-for-other-presidents

Parscale, Brad. "Trump is right: More than Facebook & Twitter, Google threatens democracy, online freedom." *USA Today.*
https://www.usatoday.com/story/opinion/2018/09/10/trump-google-youtube-search-results-biased-against-republicans-conservatives-column/1248099002/

Rothbard, Murray. *The Progressive Era.* Mises Institute. https://mises-media.s3.amazonaws.com/The%20Progressive%20Era_0.pdf

Stern, Ken. "Former NPR CEO opens up about liberal media bias." *New York Post.*
https://nypost.com/2017/10/21/the-other-half-of-america-that-the-liberal-media-doesnt-cover/

Sullivan, Meg. "Media Bias is Real, Finds UCLA Political Scientist." Free Republic. http://www.freerepublic.com/focus/f-news/1541801/posts

Thornton, Bruce. "A Brief History of Media Bias." Hoover Institution.
https://www.hoover.org/research/brief-history-media-bias

Villarreal, Daniel. "'Blatant Attack on the Constitution' Fox News Host Admits 'Stunning' Lack of Evidence Supporting Trump's Election Fraud Claims." New Civil Rights Movement.
https://www.thenewcivilrightsmovement.com/2022/06/fox-news-host-admits-stunning-lack-of-evidence-supporting-trumps-election-fraud-claims/

Weinberger, David. "The Myth That Standard Oil Was a 'Predatory Monopoly.'" Foundation for Economic Education.
https://fee.org/articles/the-myth-that-standard-oil-was-a-predatory-monopoly/

Dumb Reason #3: They Are Obsessed with LGBTQIA+ "Rights"

Ault, Alicia. "Transgender Docs Warn About Gender-Affirmative Care for Youth." WebMD.
https://www.webmd.com/sex-relationships/news/20211129/transgender-docs-gender-affirmative-care-youth

Brown, Lee. "Transgender kids OK for hormones at 14, surgery at 15, health group says." *New York Post.*
https://nypost.com/2022/06/16/trans-kids-ok-for-hormones-at-14-surgery-at-15-health-group/

Denniston, Lyle. "Opinion analysis: Marriage now open to same-sex couples." SCOTUSblog. http://www.scotusblog.com/2015/06/opinion-analysis-marriage-now-open-to-same-sex-couples/

Editors. "Attitudes on Same-Sex Marriage." Pew Research Center. http://www.pewforum.org/fact-sheet/changing-attitudes-on-gay-marriage/

Editors. "Gay Rights." History.com. https://www.history.com/topics/gay-rights/history-of-gay-rights#section_13

Fahey, Ciaran. "World Swimming Adopts New Policy for Transgender Athletes." NBC Bay Area. https://www.nbcbayarea.com/news/sports/world-swimming-adopts-new-policy-for-transgender-athletes/2923523/

Gorman, Michelle. "Gary Marriage is Legal in All 50 States: Supreme Court." *Newsweek*. https://www.newsweek.com/supreme-court-gay-marriage-legal-all-50-states-347204

Lamb, W. Scott. "20 years ago, Bill Clinton signed Defense of Marriage Act." *Washington Times*. https://www.washingtontimes.com/news/2016/sep/21/20-years-ago-bill-clinton-signed-defense-of-marria/

LaRue, Janet. "Obama Adulterates Marriage and Federalism." Townhall.com. https://townhall.com/columnists/janetmlarue/2013/03/09/obama-adulterates-marriage-and-federalism-n1529533

Salvanto, Anthony, Fred Backus, Sarah Dutton, and Jennifer De Pinto. "CBS/NYT poll: Americans divided over transgender bathroom laws, SCOTUS nomination." *CBS News.* https://www.cbsnews.com/news/cbs-poll-americans-divided-over-transgender-bathroom-laws-supreme-court/

Supreme Court. *Obergefell vs. Hodges.* SupremeCourt.gov. https://www.supremecourt.gov/opinions/14pdf/14-556_3204.pdf

Tatchell, Peter. "I've changed my mind on the gay cake row. Here's why." *The Guardian.* https://www.theguardian.com/commentisfree/2016/feb/01/gay-cake-row-i-changed-my-mind-ashers-bakery-freedom-of-conscience-religion

Wolf, Richard. "Supreme Court rules on narrow grounds for baker who refused to create same-sex couple's wedding cake." *USA Today.* https://www.usatoday.com/story/news/politics/2018/06/04/supreme-court-rules-against-gay-wedding-exemptions/1052989001/

Dumb Reason #4: They Are Preoccupied With Abortion and "Women's Rights"

Brown, Elizabeth Nolan. "Over-the-Counter Birth Control Bill Launched by Senate Republicans." *Reason.* http://reason.com/blog/2019/04/03/over-the-counter-birth-control-bill

Brown, Elizabeth Nolan. "Over-the-Counter Contraception Is Immensely Popular. But Democrats Have Doomed It." *Reason*. https://reason.com/archives/2019/01/16/deregulate-the-pill

Conover, Chris. "Are American Taxpayers Paying For Abortion?" *Forbes*. https://www.forbes.com/sites/theapothecary/2015/10/02/are-american-taxpayers-paying-for-abortion/#3c41c4406a4b

Corey, Dan. "A growing list of men accused of sexual misconduct since Weinstein." *NBC News*. https://www.nbcnews.com/storyline/sexual-misconduct/weinstein-here-s-growing-list-men-accused-sexual-misconduct-n816546

Editors. "Post-Weinstein, These Are the Powerful Men Facing Sexual Harassment Allegations." *Glamour*.

Editors. "Women Business Owner Statistics." National Association of Women Business Owners. https://www.nawbo.org/resources/women-business-owner-statistics

Follett, Chelsea. "What the Data Say About Equal Pay Day." Cato Institute. https://www.cato.org/blog/what-data-say-about-equal-pay-day

Editors. "Post-Weinstein, These Are the Powerful Men Facing Sexual Harassment Allegations." *Glamour*. https://www.glamour.com/gallery/post-weinstein-these-are-the-powerful-men-facing-sexual-harassment-allegations

Khazan, Olga. "The More Gender Equality, the Fewer Women in STEM." *The Atlantic.*
https://www.theatlantic.com/science/archive/2018/02/the-more-gender-equality-the-fewer-women-in-stem/553592/

King, Ryan. "Where every state stands on abortion in wake of Roe being overturned." *Washington Examiner.*
https://www.washingtonexaminer.com/policy/healthcare/list-where-every-state-stands-on-abortion

Lips, Karen Agness. "Don't Buy Into The Gender Pay Gap Myth." *Forbes.*
https://www.forbes.com/sites/karinagness/2016/04/12/dont-buy-into-the-gender-pay-gap-myth/#7b430ed72596

Lukas, Carrie. "There Is No Male-Female Wage Gap." *Wall Street Journal.*
https://www.wsj.com/articles/SB10001424052748704415104576250672504707048

MacDonald, Heather. "How Identity Politics Is Harming the Sciences." *City Journal Magazine.*
www.city-journal.org/html/how-identity-politics-harming-sciences-15826.html

O'Connor, Lydia. "Alabama Gov. Kay Ivey Signs Nation's Strictest Abortion Bill." HuffPost.
https://www.huffpost.com/entry/alabama-governor-signs-abortion-bill_n_5cdc8d70e4b0b4728ba29a22?ncid=engmodushpmg00000003

O'Neill, Tyler. "Supreme Court leak confirms Ruth Bader Ginsburg's prescient warning about Roe v. Wade." *New York Post*.
https://nypost.com/2022/05/04/supreme-court-leak-confirms-ruth-bader-ginsburgs-prescient-warning-about-roe-v-wade/

Polumbo, Brad. "New US Soccer fact sheet eviscerates Megan Rapinoe's 'equal pay' narrative." *Washington Examiner*.
https://www.washingtonexaminer.com/opinion/new-us-soccer-fact-sheet-eviscerates-megan-rapinoes-equal-pay-narrative

Saad, Lydia. "Americans' Abortion Views Steady Amid Gosnell Trial." Gallup.
https://news.gallup.com/poll/162374/americans-abortion-views-steady-amid-gosnell-trial.aspx

Scher, Brent. "Men Paid More Than Women in Kamala Harris's Senate Office and Campaign." *The Washington Free Beacon*.
https://freebeacon.com/politics/men-paid-more-than-women-in-kamala-harriss-senate-office-and-campaign/

Sullum, Jacob. "Here Is a State-by-State Rundown of What Will Happen Now That SCOTUS Has Freed Lawmakers To Restrict Abortion." *Reason*.
https://reason.com/2022/06/24/here-is-a-state-by-state-rundown-of-what-will-happen-now-that-scotus-has-freed-lawmakers-to-restrict-abortion/

Tobak, Steve. "The Gender Pay Gap is a Complete Myth." *CBS News.*
https://www.cbsnews.com/news/
the-gender-pay-gap-is-a-complete-myth/

Dumb Reason #5: They Worship Obama

Lewis, Michael. "The Art of Obama Worship." *Commentary.*
https://www.commentarymagazine.com/articles/
the-art-of-obama-worship/

Morrissey, Ed. "The Audacity of The Media's Obama Worship."
Hot Air.
https://hotair.com/archives/ed-morrissey/2015/02/24/
the-audacity-of-the-medias-obama-worship/

Shapiro, Ben. "Obama Worship Syndrome." Townhall.
https://townhall.com/columnists/benshapiro/2013/12/04/
obama-worship-syndrome-n1757087

Shea, Danny. Chris Matthews: "'I Felt This Thrill Going Up
My Leg' As Obama Spoke." HuffPost.
https://www.huffpost.com/entry/
chris-matthews-i-felt-thi_n_86449

Dumb Reason #6: They Hate Trump

Bandow, Doug. "Interfering In Democratic Elections: Russia
Against The U.S., But U.S. Against The World." *Forbes
Magazine.*

https://www.forbes.com/sites/dougbandow/2017/08/01/
interfering-in-democratic-elections-russia-against-the-u-s-but-u-
s-against-the-world/#6ef48dd76644

Bier, David. "Are CBP's Filthy and Inhumane Immigrant
Detention Camps Necessary?" Cato Institute.
https://www.cato.org/blog/are-cbps-filthy-inhumane-
immigrant-detention-camps-necessary

Editors. "Mueller report means the end of Trump collusion
myth." *Boston Herald*.
https://www.bostonherald.com/2019/04/19/
mueller-report-means-the-end-of-trump-collusion-myth/

Editors. "Trump and the Disabled Reporter." Liberty Alliance.
https://www.youtube.com/watch?v=dY_4BiyMnBA

Elder, Larry. "The Trump-Charlottesville 'Moral Equivalency'
Lie the Left Keeps Telling." LarryElder.com.
https://www.larryelder.com/column/the-trump-charlottesville-
moral-equivalency-lie-the-left-keeps-telling/

Graham, Jennifer. "Opinion: Will history judge Trump as
harshly as his critics on COVID-19?" *Deseret News*. https://
www.deseret.com/opinion/2022/1/4/22858917/opinion-will-
history-judge-trump-as-harshly-as-his-critics-on-covid-19-
biden-pandemic-testing

Greenfield, Daniel. "Trump Derangement Syndrome." *Front
Page Magazine*.
https://www.frontpagemag.com/fpm/264854/
trump-derangement-syndrome-daniel-greenfield

Hanson, Victor Davis. "Time to Calm Down about Trump."
National Review.
https://www.nationalreview.com/2016/03/
trump-compared-to-obama-clintons/

Harsanyi, David. "Liberals Were Very Wrong About Tax Cuts.
Again." *Reason.*
https://reason.com/2019/05/10/
liberals-were-very-wrong-about-tax-cuts-again/

Healy, Gene. "Standing on the Shoulders of Tyrants." *Reason.*
https://reason.com/2019/04/06/standing-on-the-shoulders-of-t

Heyes, J.D. "Top 20 Obama scandals: The list." *Natural News.*
https://www.naturalnews.com/041056_Obama_scandals_
Benghazi_Fast_and_Furious.html

Hill, Crystal. "In debate, Kamala Harris says she won't take a
COVID vaccine just on Trump's say-so." Yahoo! News.
https://news.yahoo.com/kamala-harris-says-she-wont-take-
covid-vaccine-just-on-trumps-sayso-020511962.html

Jarrett, Gregg. "Hillary Clinton was the mastermind behind
the Trump-Russia collusion hoax and may never face justice."
Fox News.
https://www.foxnews.com/opinion/
hillary-clinton-trump-russia-collusion-hoax-justice-gregg-jarrett

Kuklychev, Yevgeny. "Fact Check: Have More Americans
Died From COVID Under Joe Biden Than Donald Trump?"
Newsweek.

https://www.newsweek.com/fact-check-have-more-americans-died-covid-under-joe-biden-donald-trump-1661528

Levy, Robert. "The Mueller Report: FAQs." Cato Institute.
https://www.cato.org/blog/mueller-report-faqs

Lowry, Rich. "When Does Trump Get His Apology?" *National Review*.
https://www.nationalreview.com/2021/12/
when-does-trump-get-his-apology/

McGhee White, Kaylee. "Reminder: Not one person involved in Jan. 6 riot has been charged with 'insurrection.'" *The Washington Examiner*.
https://www.washingtonexaminer.com/opinion/reminder-not-one-person-involved-in-jan-6-riot-has-been-charged-with-insurrection

Snyder, Derek. "Jan. 6 wasn't an insurrection. Stop calling it what it isn't." *Springfield News-Leader*.
https://www.msn.com/en-us/news/us/jan-6-wasn-t-an-insurrection-stop-calling-it-what-it-isn-t/
ar-AASOcg8

Stark, Anna. "The seven stages of Trump Derangement Syndrome." *American Thinker*.
https://www.americanthinker.com/blog/2018/08/the_seven_stages_of_trump_derangement_syndrome.html

Dumb Reason #7: They Hate Bush

Chandrasekaran, Rajiv. "The Afghan Surge Is Over." *Foreign Policy*.
https://foreignpolicy.com/2012/09/25/the-afghan-surge-is-over/

Delman, Edward. "Obama Promised to End America's Wars—Has He?" *The Atlantic*.
https://www.theatlantic.com/international/archive/2016/03/obama-doctrine-wars-numbers/474531/

Goodman, H.A. "4,486 American Soldiers Have Died in Iraq. President Obama Is Continuing a Pointless and Deadly Quagmire." HuffPost.
https://www.huffingtonpost.com/h-a-goodman/4486-american-soldiers-ha_b_5834592.html

Heaney, Michael T. and Fabio Rojas. "The Partisan Dynamics of Contention: Demobilization of the Antiwar Movement in the United States, 2007-2009." Semantic Scholar.
https://www.semanticscholar.org/paper/The-partisan-dynamics-of-contention%3A-Demobilization-Heaney-Rojas/d8c93f40790438c6da29af016b9b6f4d857fa238

McCarthy, Andrew. "Explosive Revelation of Obama Administration Illegal Surveillance of Americans." *National Review*.
https://www.nationalreview.com/2017/05/nsa-illegal-surveillance-americans-obama-administration-abuse-fisa-court-response/

Weeks, Linton. "What Ever Happened to the Antiwar Movement?" *NPR*. https://www.npr.org/2011/04/15/135391188/whatever-happened-to-the-anti-war-movement

Dumb Reason #8: Some Are Just Immoral

Brown, Jeffrey T. "Beware the Morality of the Democrats." *American Thinker*. https://www.americanthinker.com/articles/2019/02/beware_the_morality_of_the_democrats.html

Schweppe, Jon. "The Democrats Want to Talk About Morality. Here's Why They Can't." Townhall. https://townhall.com/columnists/jonschweppe/2019/01/17/the-democrats-want-to-talk-about-morality-heres-why-they-cant-n2539210

Dumb Reason #9: They Live in Fantasy Land

Editors. "New Study: College Students Increasingly Liberal, Yet Less Politically Active." HuffPost. https://www.huffingtonpost.com/2012/01/26/student-political-views_n_1234292.html

Edsall, Thomas B. "How Did the Democrats Become Favorites of the Rich?" *The New York Times*. https://www.nytimes.com/2015/10/07/opinion/how-did-the-democrats-become-favorites-of-the-rich.html

Hayward, Steven F. "How Did the Democrats Become the Party Of The Rich?" *Forbes*.

https://www.forbes.com/sites/stevenhayward/2014/01/08/how-did-the-democrats-become-the-party-of-the-rich/#5e67a28f3f60

McElwee, Sean. "New Evidence That The Rich Are More Conservative Than the Rest." HuffPost. https://www.huffingtonpost.com/sean-mcelwee/new-evidence-that-the-ric_b_7153396.html

Soffen, Kim. "Just How Liberal Are College Students?" *Harvard Political Review.* http://harvardpolitics.com/harvard/just-liberal-college-students/

Welch, Matt. "Democrats Hate Wealthy Candidates…When They're Not Democrats." *Reason.* http://reason.com/blog/2019/01/31/democrats-hate-wealthy-candidateswhen-th

Dumb Reason #10: They Are Jealous

Bourne, Ryan. "Capitalism's Critics Need to Be Told About Its 200 Years of Success." Cato Institute. https://www.cato.org/publications/commentary/capitalisms-critics-need-be-told-about-its-200-years-success

Brooks, Chad. "How Most Millionaires Got Rich." *Business News Daily.* https://www.businessnewsdaily.com/2871-how-most-millionaires-got-rich.html

De Rugy, Veronique. "Democratic Wealth Tax Proposals Demonstrate Economic Ignorance." *Reason.*

https://reason.com/2019/10/24/democratic-wealth-tax-proposals-demonstrate-economic-ignorance/

Early, John F. "Reassessing the Facts about Inequality, Poverty, and Redistribution." Cato Institute. https://www.cato.org/publications/policy-analysis/reassessing-facts-about-inequality-poverty-redistribution#full

Edwards, Chris and Ryan Bourne. "Exploring Wealth Inequality." Cato Institute. https://www.cato.org/publications/policy-analysis/exploring-wealth-inequality

Edwards, Chris. "Government Expansion Increases Wealth Inequality." Cato Institute. https://www.cato.org/blog/government-expansion-increases-wealth-inequality

Hertel-Fernandez, Alexander and Theda Skocpol. "Five Myths About the Koch Brothers — And Why It Matters to Set Them Straight." BillMoyers.com. https://billmoyers.com/story/five-myths-about-the-koch-network-and-why-it-matters-to-set-them-straight/

Keller, Bill. "Is Charles Koch a Closet Liberal?" *Newsweek*. https://www.newsweek.com/charles-koch-closet-liberal-418860

Lee, Patrice J. "Americans Still Believe in the American Dream." Independent Women's Forum. http://www.iwf.org/blog/2795416/Americans-Still-Believe-in-the-American-Dream

Perry, Mark J. "America's Record Middle-Class Earnings Exposes the 'Imaginary Hobgoblin' of Income Inequality." Foundation for Economic Education. https://fee.org/articles/americas-record-middle-class-earnings-exposes-the-imaginary-hobgoblin-of-income-inequality/

Tanner, Michael D. "Five Myths about Economic Inequality in America." Cato Institute. https://www.cato.org/publications/policy-analysis/five-myths-about-economic-inequality-america

Tanner, Michael D. "The Income-Inequality Myth." Cato Institute. https://www.cato.org/publications/commentary/incomeinequality-myth

Dumb Reason #11: They Have Visions of Western Europe

Editors. "List of countries by homeless population." Wikipedia. https://en.wikipedia.org/wiki/List_of_countries_by_homeless_population

Editors. "Thousands in Britain left to go blind due to eye surgery rationing: Report." *The Straits Times.* https://www.straitstimes.com/world/europe/thousands-in-britain-left-to-go-blind-due-to-eye-surgery-rationing-report

Foster, Dawn. "Homelessness and housing problems reach crisis point in all EU countries – except Finland." *The Guardian.* https://www.theguardian.com/housing-network/2017/mar/21/homelessness-housing-problems-crisis-point-all-eu-countries-except-finland

Gobry, Pascal-Emmanuel. "Attention Bernie Sanders: Europe gave up on its socialist paradise years ago." *The Week*. https://theweek.com/articles/600512/attention-bernie-sanders-europe-gave-socialist-paradise-years-ago

Hays, Charlotte. "Bipartisan Proposals on Drug Price Controls Threaten Innovation." Independent Women's Forum. http://iwf.org/blog/2808372/Bipartisan-Proposals-on-Drug-Price-Controls-Threaten-Innovation

Herzlinger, Regina E. and Bacchus Barua. "Europe's Alternative to Medicare for All." *Wall Street Journal*. https://www.wsj.com/articles/europes-alternative-to-medicare-for-all-11555457596

Johnson, Rev. Ben. "Single-Payer Healthcare Topples Nordic Government." Intellectual Takeout. http://intellectualtakeout.org/article/single-payer-healthcare-topples-nordic-government

Lowry, Rich. "Sorry, Bernie — Scandinavia is no socialist paradise after all." *New York Post*. https://nypost.com/2015/10/19/sorry-bernie-scandinavia-is-no-socialist-paradise-after-all/

Madden, Heather. "Medicare For All Would Make a Bad Situation Even Worse." Independent Women's Forum. https://www.iwf.org/2020/03/16/medicare-for-all-would-make-a-bad-situation-even-worse/

Magness, Phillip W. "Even Swedish Socialism was Violent." American Institute for Economic Research.

https://www.aier.org/article/even-swedish-socialism-was-violent

Malcolm, Candice. "The Pitfalls of Single-Payer Health Care: Canada's Cautionary Tale." *National Review.*
https://www.nationalreview.com/2017/04/
canada-single-payer-health-care-system-failures-cautionary-tale/

Matthews, Chris. "What the Left Gets Wrong About Scandinavia." *Fortune.*
https://fortune.com/2016/01/26/
democrat-bernie-sanders-scandinavia-socialism/

McDonald, Kelly. "Scandinavia Isn't A Socialist Paradise." The Federalist.
http://thefederalist.com/2015/08/11/
scandinavia-isnt-a-socialist-paradise/

Moffit, Robert, Friedrich Breyer, Philippe Manière, Paul Belien, David Green, and Johan Hjertgvist. "Perspectives on the European Health Care Systems: Some Lessons for America." Heritage Foundation.
https://www.heritage.org/health-care-reform/report/
perspectives-the-european-health-care-systems-some-lessons-
america

Moffit, Robert. "Medicare's Financial Condition Is Getting Worse. Here's What Trump and Congress Can Do." *The Daily Signal.*
https://www.dailysignal.com/2019/02/20/medicares-financial-
condition-is-getting-worse-heres-what-trump-and-congress-
can-do/

Sarmiento, Mabel. "The Revolution Annihilated Oil Workers." Caracas Chronicles. https://www.caracaschronicles.com/2019/10/11/the-revolution-annihilated-oil-workers/

Simon, Johnson. "Scottish patients 'forced to wait more than two years' despite Nicola Sturgeon's treatment guarantee." *The Telegraph.* https://www.telegraph.co.uk/politics/2019/01/04/scottish-patients-forced-wait-two-years-despite-nicola-sturgeons/

Swanson, Ana. "Why Denmark isn't the utopian fantasy Bernie Sanders describes." *The Washington Post.* https://www.washingtonpost.com/news/wonk/wp/2015/11/03/why-denmark-isnt-the-utopian-fantasy-bernie-sanders-describes/

Wollstein, Jarret B. "National Health Insurance: A Medical Disaster." Foundation for Economic Education. https://fee.org/articles/national-health-insurance-a-medical-disaster/

Dumb Reason #12: They Are Tribalists

Albright, Logan. "Can We Stop Pretending Democrats Care About Black People, Immigrants?" FreedomWorks. http://www.freedomworks.org/content/can-we-stop-pretending-democrats-care-about-black-people-immigrants

Bloom Jackson, Kimberly. "The Secret Racist History of the Democratic Party." *American Thinker.* https://www.americanthinker.com/articles/2016/05/the_secret_racist_history_of_the_democratic_party.html

Elder, Larry. "Criminal Behavior, Not Racism, Explains 'Racial Disparities' in Crime Stats." RealClear Politics. https://www.realclearpolitics.com/articles/2018/06/28/criminal_behavior_not_racism_explains_racial_disparities_in_crime_stats_137370.html#!

Elder, Larry. "Crippling children by selling them racism." *Washington Examiner.* https://www.washingtonexaminer.com/crippling-children-by-selling-them-racism

Elder, Larry. "Five Myths of the 'Racist' Criminal Justice System." Townhall. https://townhall.com/columnists/larryelder/2012/04/19/creators-oped-n1141269

Elder, Larry. "The Truth About the Central Park Five." The Larry Elder Show. https://youtu.be/hwRQztpF6qU
(also also referenced in a previous chapter)

Krogstad, Jens Manuel and Mark Hugo Lopez. "Hispanic Voters in the 2014 Election: Democratic Advantage Remains, but Republicans Improve Margin in Some States." Pew Research Center. http://www.pewhispanic.org/2014/11/07/hispanic-voters-in-the-2014-election/

Shapiro, Ben. "6 Leftist Myths About The Criminal Justice System That Get Blacks Killed." The Daily Wire. https://www.dailywire.com/news/4847/6-leftist-myths-about-criminal-justice-system-get-ben-shapiro

Sowell, Thomas. "Lessons From the Past." Creators.com.
https://www.creators.com/read/thomas-sowell/01/19/
lessons-from-the-past

Sung Park, Jay. "The Myth of Institutional Racism." *Merion West.*
https://merionwest.com/2017/08/19/
the-myth-of-institutional-racism/

Dumb Reason #13: They Hate the Constitution

Carter, Joe. "Justice Scalia explains why the 'living Constitution' is a threat to America." Acton Institute.
https://blog.acton.org/archives/101616-justice-scalia-explains-
why-the-living-constitution-is-a-threat-to-america.html

Harsanyi, David. "Do Democrats Care About The Constitution Anymore? It Sure Doesn't Look Like It." The Federalist.
https://thefederalist.com/2016/06/17/
do-democrats-care-about-the-constitution-anymore/

Hobbs, Killian. "The Constitution and Beto's Question: A Libertarian Answer." Being Libertarian.
https://beinglibertarian.com/
the-constitution-and-betos-question-a-libertarian-answer/

Kraychik, Robert. "Feinstein: Constitution A 'Living Document;' 'Originalism… Very Troubling.'" DailyWire.com.
https://www.dailywire.com/news/feinstein-constitution-living-
document-originalism-robert-kraychik

Dumb Reason #14: Some Just Want to Be "Cool"

Early, John F. "Reassessing the Facts about Inequality, Poverty, and Redistribution." Cato Institute. https://www.cato.org/publications/policy-analysis/ reassessing-facts-about-inequality-poverty-redistribution#full

Marshall, Serena. "Obama Has Deported More People Than Any Other President." *ABC News.* https://abcnews.go.com/Politics/ obamas-deportation-policy-numbers/story?id=41715661

Shipley, Kelci. "11 Times Barack Obama Was the Coolest President." *MTV News.* http://www.mtv.com/news/1887006/ happy-birthday-barack-obama/

Dumb Reason #15: They Hate Conservatives

Healy, Gene. "Standing on the Shoulders of Tyrants." *Reason.* https://reason.com/2019/04/06/standing-on-the-shoulders-of-t

Newport, Frank. "How Many Highly Religious Conservative Republicans Are There?" Gallup. https://news.gallup.com/opinion/polling-matters/182210/ highly-religious-conservative-republicans.aspx

Shaw, Maureen. "The majority of America is now pro-choice." ThinkProgress. https://thinkprogress.org/ pro-choice-america-majority-d8963029ae45/

Sides, John. "White Christian America is dying." *Washington Post*.
https://www.washingtonpost.com/news/monkey-cage/
wp/2016/08/15/white-christian-america-is-dying/

Tomlin, Gregory. "Socially conservative Republicans at 10-year low, Gallup says." *Christian Examiner*.
https://www.christianexaminer.com/article/socially-
conservative-republicans-at-10-year-low-gallup-says/49048.htm

Wassil, Cameron. "Yes, I Hate Republicans And No, I Will Not Apologize." The Odyssey Online.
https://www.theodysseyonline.com/
hate-republicans-hate-hatred

Dumb Reason #16: They Don't Want You Touching Their Handouts

Amadeo, Kimberly. "Current Federal Mandatory Spending." The Balance.
https://www.thebalance.com/
current-federal-mandatory-spending-3305772

Cox, Jeff. "What's the worst that could happen? 7 debt-default doomsday scenarios." *NBC News*.
https://www.nbcnews.com/businessmain/whats-worst-could-
happen-7-debt-default-doomsday-scenarios-8C11366851

Edwards, Chris. "The Problems with Federal Government Debt." Downsizing the Federal Government.
https://www.downsizinggovernment.org/federal-debt

Foster, J.D. "The Many Real Dangers of Soaring National Debt." The Heritage Foundation.
https://www.heritage.org/budget-and-spending/report/the-many-real-dangers-soaring-national-debt

Matthews, Merrill. "We've Crossed The Tipping Point; Most Americans Now Receive Government Benefits." *Forbes.*
https://www.forbes.com/sites/merrillmatthews/2014/07/02/weve-crossed-the-tipping-point-most-americans-now-receive-government-benefits/#4434f0643e6c

Stossel, John. "Private Charity Beats One-Size-Fits-All Government." *Reason.*
https://reason.com/2020/12/02/private-charity-beats-one-size-fits-all-government/

Welch, Sharpel. "Government Help Will Never Be Enough." City Journal.
https://www.city-journal.org/government-benefits

Dumb Reason #17: They Are Part of the "Mob"

Abram, Ted. "A Referendum on the Failure of the Progressive Era - Part I: Progressives Pervert Our Constitution." FreedomWorks.
http://www.freedomworks.org/content/referendum-failure-progressive-era-part-i-progressives-pervert-our-constitution

Fulton, Joshua. "Welfare before the Welfare State." Mises Institute.
https://mises.org/library/welfare-welfare-state

Rothbard, Murray. *The Progressive Era*. Mises Institute. https://mises-media.s3.amazonaws.com/The%20 Progressive%20Era_0.pdf
(also also referenced in a previous chapter)

Scandlen, Greg. The Federalist. "Mutual Aid Societies: It's Amazing What People Can Do Together." http://thefederalist.com/2014/08/27/ mutual-aid-societies-its-amazing-what-people-can-do-together/

Dumb Reason #18: They Seek a Utopia

Duclos, Susan. "All It Took Was Radical Liberal Policies to Turn U.S. 'Utopian' Cities Into Hell-Holes - This Is What They Want For America." All News Pipeline. http://allnewspipeline.com/Utopia_Into_Hell_Radical_Lib_ Policies.php

Ebeling, Richard M. "'Liberal Socialism' is Another False Utopia." Foundation for Economic Education. https://fee.org/articles/liberal-socialism-is-another-false-utopia/

Editors. "Democrat's Utopia: Racism, Riots, Economic Ruin and Poison Water." Truth and Action. http://www.truthandaction.org/ democratic-utopia-racism-riots-economic-ruin-poison-water/

Geraghty, Jim. "Why We Can't Have Wakanda." *National Review*. https://www.nationalreview.com/2018/02/ wakanda-utopia-impossible-blame-human-nature/

Mosbacher, Mica. "Even A 'Wealth Tax' Wouldn't Pay For The Democrats' Utopia." Townhall. https://townhall.com/columnists/micamosbacher/2019/02/22/even-a-wealth-tax-wouldnt-pay-for-the-democrats-utopia-n2542066

Riedl, Brian. "The Magical Thinking Behind Warren's Medicare for All Plan." The Manhattan Institute. https://www.manhattan-institute.org/the-magical-thinking-behind-warrens-medicare-for-all-plan

Dumb Reason #19: They Are Shortsighted Thinkers

Blankley, Bethany. "Report: Benefit, job cuts resulting from minimum wage hike offset increased pay." The Center Square. https://www.thecentersquare.com/national/report-benefit-job-cuts-resulting-from-minimum-wage-hike-offset/article_82f29370-e6a5-11e9-9e1d-87e6e42e0fd2.amp.html

Boehm, Eric. "Target Employees Won The 'Fight For $15' but Weren't Ready for the Trade-Offs." *Reason.* https://reason.com/2019/10/21/target-15-bucks-per-hour-didnt-work-out/

Coleman, Hank. "The Negative Effects of Raising Minimum Wage in America." Money Q&A. https://moneyqanda.com/effects-of-raising-minimum-wage/

De Rugy, Veronique. "Democratic Wealth Tax Proposals Demonstrate Economic Ignorance." *Reason.* https://reason.com/2019/10/24/democratic-wealth-tax-proposals-demonstrate-economic-ignorance/

(also also referenced in a previous chapter)

De Rugy, Veronique. "Plans by Warren and Sanders Neglect Logic, Math, and Honesty." *Reason.*
https://reason.com/2019/11/07/
plans-by-warren-and-sanders-neglect-logic-math-and-honesty/

Edwards, Chris. "Negative Effects of Minimum Wages." Cato Institute.
https://www.cato.org/blog/negative-effects-minimum-wage

Elder, Larry. "If $15 minimum wage is such a good idea, why did AOC's bar close down?" Toronto Sun.
https://torontosun.com/opinion/columnists/elder-if-15-minimum-wage-is-such-a-good-idea-why-did-aocs-bar-close-down

Engelberg, Alfred B. "How Government Policy Promotes High Drug Prices." Health Affairs.
https://www.healthaffairs.org/do/10.1377/
hblog20151029.051488/full/

Greenhut, Steven. "There's No Such Thing as 'Free Money' or Meaningless Deficits." *Reason.*
https://reason.com/2019/08/02/
theres-no-such-thing-as-free-money-or-meaningless-deficits/

Stossel, John. "Why Should Government Be Involved in Medicine at All?" *Reason.*
https://reason.com/archives/2012/06/14/
why-should-government-be-involved-in-med

Tu, Janet I. "UW study finds Seattle's minimum wage is costing jobs Seattle Times." *Seattle Times*.
https://www.seattletimes.com/business/
uw-study-finds-seattles-minimum-wage-is-costing-jobs/

Dumb Reason #20: They Seek Payback

Editors. "How Americans View Government." Pew Research Center.
http://www.people-press.org/1998/03/10/
how-americans-view-government/

Editors. "Public Opinions on Social Security." National Academy of Social Insurance.
https://www.nasi.org/learn/social-security/
public-opinions-social-security

Woodhill, Louis. "Rising Wealth Inequality Is Bad, But Liberal 'Solutions' Are Much Worse." *Forbes*.
https://www.forbes.com/sites/louiswoodhill/2013/10/09/
rising-wealth-inequality-is-bad-but-liberal-solutions-are-much-
worse/#71e50c61338fj

Dumb Reason #21: They Are Hippies Forever

Bernstein, Andrew. "Black Innovators and Entrepreneurs Under Capitalism." Foundation for Economic Education.
https://fee.org/articles/
black-innovators-and-entrepreneurs-under-capitalism/

Editors. "Hippie." Encyclopædia Britannica.
https://www.britannica.com/topic/hippie

Editors. "Jim Crow Laws." History.
https://www.history.com/topics/early-20th-century-us/
jim-crow-laws

Editors. "Jim Crow Laws." National Park Service.
https://www.nps.gov/malu/learn/education/jim_crow_laws.htm

Elder, Larry. "Blacks, Banks and 'Institutional Racism.'"
Creators.
https://www.creators.com/read/larry-elder/07/07/
blacks-banks-and-institutional-racism

Richardson, Valerie. "Police kill more whites than blacks, but
minority deaths generate more outrage." *The Washington Times*.
https://www.washingtontimes.com/news/2015/apr/21/
police-kill-more-whites-than-blacks-but-minority-d/

Sowell, Thomas. "Does Black Success Matter?" Creators.
https://www.creators.com/read/thomas-sowell/08/16/
does-black-success-matter

Dumb Reason #22: They Are "Environmentalists"

Bailey, Ronald. "Capitalism Is the Key to Fixing Climate
Change." *Reason*.
https://reason.com/2019/09/20/
capitalism-is-the-key-to-fixing-climate-change/

Bailey, Ronald. "Is Climate Change Making Hurricanes More
Destructive?" *Reason*.
https://reason.com/blog/2019/01/17/hurricane-losses

Bailey, Ronald. "The Green New Deal Is Anti-Democratic." *Reason*.
https://reason.com/2019/04/07/the-green-new-deal-is-anti-dem

Boehm, Eric. "Private Companies Are Paying to Keep Yellowstone Clean During Shutdown." *Reason*.
https://reason.com/blog/2019/01/07/
private-companies-yellowstone-shutdown

Britschgi, Christian. "Justin Trudeau Uses 9-Year-Old's Straw Stats To Sell Ban on Single-Use Plastics." Reason.
https://reason.com/2019/06/10/justin-trudeau-uses-9-year-olds-
straw-stats-to-sell-ban-on-single-use-plastics/

Bryce, Robert. "The Antithesis of Green." *National Review*.
https://www.nationalreview.com/2019/01/
green-new-deal-renewable-energy-cannot-meet-needs/

Dalmia, Shikha. "Flint's water crisis isn't a failure of austerity. It's a failure of government." *The Week*.
https://theweek.com/articles/600101

De Rugy, Veronique. "Will Uprisings Thwart Green Central Planners?" *Reason*.
https://reason.com/archives/2018/12/13/
will-uprisings-thwart-green-central-plan

Editors. "Our Nation's Air." Environmental Protection Agency.
https://gispub.epa.gov/air/trendsreport/2017/#growth

Gillespie, Nick. "Think Globally, Shame Constantly: The Rise of Greta Thunberg Environmentalism." *Reason*.

https://reason.com/2019/09/24/think-globally-shame-constantly-the-rise-of-greta-thunberg-environmentalism/

Grimberg, Jenny. "The Wrong Solutions to Fighting Climate Change." Being Libertarian. https://beinglibertarian.com/ the-wrong-solutions-to-fighting-climate-change/

Grimes, David Robert. "Why it's time to dispel the myths about nuclear power." *The Guardian.* https://www.theguardian.com/science/blog/2016/apr/11/ time-dispel-myths-about-nuclear-power-chernobyl-fukushima

Gunlock, Julie. "California's War on Cleanliness." Independent Women's Forum. https://www.iwf.org/2019/04/18/californias-war-on-cleanliness/

Heath, Hadley. "Well-Intended, Expensive Green New Deal Plan Has Problems." Independent Women's Forum. http://iwf.org/blog/2808350/ Well-Intended,-Expensive-Green-New-Deal-Plan-Has-Problems

Hoekstra, Kathy. "Fracking vs. Flint: The EPA has out-of-whack priorities." *Washington Examiner.* https://www.washingtonexaminer.com/ fracking-vs-flint-the-epa-has-out-of-whack-priorities

Lesser, Jonathan A. "The Drive to Make New York 'Zero Carbon' Is Insane." *New York Post.* https://www.manhattan-institute.org/html/ new-york-insane-zero-carbon

Lomborg, Bjorn. "Climate change activists are focused on all the wrong solutions." New York Post. https://nypost.com/2019/10/12/climate-change-activists-are-focused-on-all-the-wrong-solutions/

Lomborg, Bjorn. "The media got it all wrong on the new US climate report." *New York Post.* https://nypost.com/2018/11/28/the-media-got-it-all-wrong-on-the-new-us-climate-report/

Lomborg, Bjorn. "Truth is the First Casualty of Global Warming." Project Syndicate. https://www.project-syndicate.org/commentary/climate-change-self-defeating-alarmism-by-bjorn-lomborg-2018-12

Munger, Michael. "For Most Things, Recycling Harms the Environment." American Institute for Economic Research." https://aier.org/article/for-most-things-recycling-harms-the-environment/

Murphy, James. "The Myth of the Paris Climate Accord." The New American. https://www.thenewamerican.com/tech/environment/item/28621-the-myth-of-the-paris-climate-accord

Nace, Trevor. "The World's Largest Ocean Cleanup Has Officially Begun." *Forbes.* https://www.forbes.com/sites/trevornace/2018/09/10/the-worlds-largest-ocean-cleanup-has-officially-begun/#6b90b6732738

Perry, Mark J. "The Environmental Costs of Renewable Energy Are Staggering." Foundation for Economic Education. https://fee.org/articles/ the-environmental-costs-of-renewable-energy-are-staggering/

Ryder, Taryn. "Harrison Ford called out for using 'private jets' after speech at UN Climate Action Summit." Yahoo. https://www.yahoo.com/entertainment/harrison-ford-called-out-for-using-private-jets-after-speech-at-un-climate-action-summit-001129311.html

Schwartz, Joel. "The Air Pollution Con Game." Cato Institute. https://www.cato.org/publications/commentary/ air-pollution-con-game

Shellenberger, Michael. "The Only Green New Deals That Have Ever Worked Were Done With Nuclear, Not Renewables." *Forbes.* https://forbes.com/sites/michaelshellenberger/2019/02/08/the-only-green-new-deals-that-have-ever-worked-were-done-with-nuclear-not-renewables/#1e3b7370798e

Shellenberger, Michael. "Why HBO's 'Chernobyl' Gets Nuclear So Wrong." *Forbes.* https://www. forbes.com/sites/michaelshellenberger/2019/06/06/ why-hbos-chernobyl-gets-nuclear-so-wrong

Soave, Robby. "Democrats Forget the Flint Water Crisis Was Caused by a Bold New Infrastructure Plan." *Reason.* https://reason.com/2019/07/30/ flint-water-crisis-democrat-debate-infrastructure/

Stossel, John. "Banning Straws." Townhall.
https://townhall.com/columnists/johnstossel/2018/07/18/
banning-straws-n2501183

Stossel, John. "Green Tyranny." Creators.
https://www.creators.com/read/john-stossel/04/13/
green-tyranny

Taylor, James. "Updated NASA Data: Global Warming Not
Causing Any Polar Ice Retreat." Frontiers of Freedom.
https://www.ff.org/updated-nasa-data-global-warming-not-
causing-any-polar-ice-retreat/

Dumb Reason #23: They Follow in Their Parents' Footsteps

Chang, Alvin. "Your politics aren't just passed down from your
parents. This cartoon explains what actually happens." Vox.
https://www.vox.com/policy-and-politics/2016/11/22/13714556/
parent-child-politics-research-cartoon

Editors. "What Factors Shape Political Attitudes?" U.S.
History.
http://www.ushistory.org/gov/4b.asp

Patterson, Te-Erika. "Do Children Just Take Their Parents'
Political Beliefs? It's Not That Simple." The Atlantic.
https://www.theatlantic.com/politics/archive/2014/05/
parents-political-beliefs/361462/

Dumb Reason #24: They've Never Run a Business

Blake, Arron. "Obama's 'You didn't build that' problem The Washington Post."
https://www.washingtonpost.com/blogs/the-fix/post/obamas-you-didnt-build-that-problem/2012/07/18/gJQAJxyotW_blog.html?utm_term=.cc5df9618720

Brown Calder, Vanessa. "Good Intentions and Bad News: Minimum-Wage Edition." Cato Institute.
https://www.cato.org/publications/commentary/good-intentions-bad-news-minimum-wage-edition

Fiedler, Katharina. "90% of American workers don't own their own business, Rick Santorum says." Politifact.
https://www.politifact.com/truth-o-meter/statements/2015/apr/13/rick-santorum/90-american-workers-dont-own-their-own-business-ri/

Gillespie, Nick. "New York Passes Minimum Wage Law for Uber, Lyft Drivers, Hikes Costs to Riders." *Reason*.
https://reason.com/blog/2018/12/05/new-york-passes-minimum-wage-law-for-ube

Hoover, Kent. "10 regulations that give small business owners the worst headaches." The Business Journals.
https://www.bizjournals.com/bizjournals/washingtonbureau/2016/04/10-regulations-that-give-small-business-owners-the.html

Monticello, Justin. "This Insane Battle To Block a New Apartment Building Explains Why San Francisco and Other Cities Are So Expensive." Reason. https://reason.com/reasontv/2018/12/27/ san-francisco-mission-housing-crisis

Nazar, Jason. "16 Surprising Statistics About Small Businesses." *Forbes.* https://www.forbes.com/sites/jasonnazar/2013/09/09/16- surprising-statistics-about-small-businesses/#3c8fa65b5ec8

Tu, Janet I. "UW study finds Seattle's minimum wage is costing jobs Seattle Times." Seattle Times. https://www.seattletimes.com/business/ uw-study-finds-seattles-minimum-wage-is-costing-jobs/ (also referenced in a previous chapter)

Wilson, Mark. "The Negative Effects of Minimum Wage Laws." Cato Institute. https://www.cato.org/publications/policy-analysis/ negative-effects-minimum-wage-laws

Dumb Reason #25: They Are Anti-Gun

Carno, Laura. "Women Testify Against Proposed Congressional Assault Weapon Ban." Independent Women's Forum. http://iwf.org/blog/2810678/Women-Testify-Against-Proposed- Congressional-Assault-Weapon-Ban

Davies, Logan. "We Need a Realistic Discussion About Firearms." Being Libertarian.

https://beinglibertarian.com/
we-need-a-realistic-discussion-about-firearms/

Doherty, Brian. "Media Reports Australians 'Handed In'
57,000 Guns Last Year; 37,000 of Them Essentially Handed
Right Back." *Reason.*
https://reason.com/blog/2018/03/01/
media-reports-australians-handed-in-5700

Elder, Larry. "Evidence Shows Gun Buybacks Don't Work."
Larry Elder Show.
https://youtu.be/A1GNbse4QYA

Elder, Larry. "How Many Lives Are Saved by Guns -- and Why
Don't Gun Controllers Care?" Real Clear Politics.
https://www.realclearpolitics.com/articles/2018/03/01/how_
many_lives_are_saved_by_guns_--_and_why_dont_gun_
controllers_care_136408.html#!

Elder, Larry. "Yes, Gun Control Advocates Do Want to Take
Our Guns — Just Listen To Them." Investor's Business Daily.
https://www.investors.com/politics/columnists/yes-gun-control-
advocates-do-want-to-take-our-guns-just-listen-to-them-larry-
elder/

Kopel, David B. "The Costs and Consequences of Gun
Control." Cato Institute.
https://www.cato.org/publications/policy-analysis/
costs-consequences-gun-control

Kopel, David B. and Vincent Harinam. "Britain's Failed Weapons-Control Laws Show Why the Second Amendment Matters." *National Review.* https://www.nationalreview.com/2018/08/ britain-failed-weapons-control-laws-curb-self-defense-rights/

Libresco, Leah. "The depressing truth about gun control." *The New York Post.* https://nypost.com/2017/10/05/ the-depressing-truth-about-gun-control/

Lott, John R. "After Virginia Beach shooting, Dems seek ban on 'silencers' that don't make guns silent." *Fox News.* https://www.foxnews.com/opinion/ john-lott-virginia-beach-suppressors

Mehta, Varad. "The Australia Gun Control Fallacy." The Federalist. http://thefederalist.com/2015/06/25/ the-australia-gun-control-fallacy/

Stossel, John. "Myths About Gun Control." Real Clear Politics. https://www.realclearpolitics.com/Commentary/ com-10_19_05_JS.html

Sullum, Jacob. "A Massacre Is Not an Argument." Reason. https://reason.com/ archives/2017/10/04/a-massacre-is-not-an-argument

Sullum, Jacob. "After Uvalde, Politicians Push Irrelevant Gun Control Proposals." Reason. https://reason.com/2022/07/02/ after-uvalde-irrelevant-gun-control-proposals/

Dumb Reason #26: They Are Slaves to Peer Pressure

Chozick, Amy. "Can Peer Pressure Defeat Trump?" *The New York Times*.
https://www.nytimes.com/2019/02/22/sunday-review/2020-election-voting-apps.html

Navarro, Claire. "Social Citizens: How Peer Networks Influence Elections." Hold That Thought.
https://artsci.wustl.edu/ampersand/
social-citizens-how-peer-networks-influence-elections

Snibbe, Kris. "Peer pressure in politics." *The Harvard Gazette.*
https://news.harvard.edu/gazette/story/2012/10/
peer-pressure-in-politics/

Dumb Reason #27: They Feel Guilty

Armstrong, Ari. "'White Privilege': Myths and Facts." *The Objective Standard.*
https://www.theobjectivestandard.com/2014/06/
white-privilege-myths-facts/

Bernard, Claston. "Disgusting: Liberals, White Guilt and Race Hustling." New Wright Network.
https://newrightnetwork.com/2019/06/liberals-white-guilt-race-hustling.html/

Goldberg, Bernard. "White Liberals and the New Racism."
BernardGoldberg.
https://bernardgoldberg.com/white-liberals-new-racism/

Prager, Dennis. "The Fallacy of 'White Privilege.'" *The National Review.*
https://www.nationalreview.com/2016/02/
white-privilege-myth-reality/

Steele, Shelby. "The Exhaustion of American Liberalism." *Wall Street Journal.*
https://www.wsj.com/articles/
the-exhaustion-of-american-liberalism-1488751826

Dumb Reason #28: They're Immigrants Who Never Learned About Our History

Cillizza, Chris. "Americans know literally nothing about the Constitution." *CNN.*
https://www.cnn.com/2017/09/13/politics/poll-constitution/
index.html

Editors. "Americans Are Poorly Informed About Basic Constitutional Provisions." Annenberg Public Policy Center.
https://www.annenbergpublicpolicycenter.org/americans-are-
poorly-informed-about-basic-constitutional-provisions/

Hentoff, Nat. "Our Constitution: How Many of Us Know It?" Cato Institute.
https://www.cato.org/publications/commentary/
our-constitution-how-many-us-know-it

Naseem, Saba. "How Much U.S. History Do Americans Actually Know? Less Than You Think." Smithsonian.
https://www.smithsonianmag.com/history/how-much-us-
history-do-americans-actually-know-less-you-think-180955431/

Rudalevige, Andrew. "Too many Americans know too little about the Constitution. Here's how you can fix that." *Washington Post*.
https://www.washingtonpost.com/news/monkey-cage/wp/2017/06/27/too-many-americans-know-too-little-about-the-constitution-heres-how-you-can-fix-that/

Dumb Reason #29: They're Teachers

DeAngelis, Corey. "Ill Democratic Omens in Education Polls." *The Wall Street Journal*.
https://www.wsj.com/articles/ill-democratic-omens-in-education-polls-teachers-union-randi-weingarten-gop-trust-parents-schools-aft-11658521717

Domanico, Ray. "The South Bronx School That Outscores the Suburbs." City Journal.
https://www.city-journal.org/harlem-success-academy-charter-school

Editors. "How Did Government Get So Involved in Education?" Alliance for the Separate of School & State.
https://schoolandstate.com/?page_id=56

Editors. "Why does the L.A. teachers union want to limit the options for poor children?" *The Washington Post*.
https://www.washingtonpost.com/opinions/why-does-the-la-teachers-union-want-to-limit-the-options-for-poor-children/2019/01/17/eb4a0946-19d5-11e9-8813-cb9dec761e73_story.html?noredirect=on&utm_term=.0c7e28dd58a0

Feltscher Stepman, Inez. "Behind the Los Angeles Teachers' Strike." Independent Women's Forum. https://www.iwf.org/2019/01/14/ behind-the-los-angeles-teachers-strike/

Feltscher Stepman, Inez. "Parents Have a Right to Educational Options for Their Kids." The Daily Caller. http://iwf.org/news/2808381/Parents-Have-a-Right-to-Educational-Options-for-Their-Kid s?fbclid=IwAR0wMcVjxGrhpdKM3ux06e9 Dgw_LKwCU5_YgiZYAH2klioBeGD57TMobt3g

Edwards, Chris. "Which States Provide High Quality Schools at Low Cost?" Cato Institute. https://www.cato.org/blog/ which-states-provide-high-quality-schools-low-cost

Griffith, David. "Rising Tide: Charter School Market Share and Student Achievement." Thomas B. Fordham Institute. https://fordhaminstitute.org/national/research/ rising-tide-charter-market-share

McCluskey, Neal. "Cutting Federal Aid for K-12 Education." Downsizing the Federal Government. https://www.downsizinggovernment.org/ education/k-12-education-subsidies

McGee, Josh B. "Teachers strike for higher pay because administration and benefits take too much money." *USA Today*. https://www.usatoday.com/story/opinion/2019/02/18/denver-teachers-strike-higher-pay-growing-retirement-benefit-costs-column/2846157002/

Ohanian, Lee E. "LA teachers strike to preserve their ruinous monopoly." The Hill. https://thehill.com/opinion/education/425831-la-teachers-strike-to-preserve-their-ruinous-monopoly

Riley, Jason L. "Teachers Unions Don't Really Strike for 'the Kids.'" Manhattan Institute. https://www.manhattan-institute.org/html/teachers-unions-not-striking-for-kids

Sexton, John. "Washington Post Editorial Board Slams LA Teacher's Union." Hot Air. https://hotair.com/archives/2019/01/18/washington-post-editorial-board-slams-la-teachers-union/

Strauss, Valerie. "Why the L.A. teachers strike is so uncomfortable for so many Democrats." *The Washington Post.* https://www.washingtonpost.com/education/2019/01/17/why-la-teachers-strike-is-so-uncomfortable-so-many-democrats/

Winters, Marcus A. "To Determine the Real Difference Between District and Charter Schools, Research Must Do More Than Just Compare Test Scores." Manhattan Institute. https://www.manhattan-institute.org/real-difference-district-and-charter-schools-more-than-test-scores

Dumb Reason #30: They Blame Capitalism and Free Markets

Abram, Ted. "A Referendum on the Failure of the Progressive Era - Part I: Progressives Pervert Our Constitution." FreedomWorks.

http://www.freedomworks.org/content/referendum-failure-pro-gressive-era-part-i-progressives-pervert-our-constitution (also referenced in a previous chapter)

Alger, Vicki E. "It's Time to Admit the Feds Are Making Poverty Worse--Not Better." The Daily Caller. https://www.iwf.org/2019/01/29/its-time-to-admit-the-feds-are-making-poverty-worse-not-better/

Casella, Tony. "Undeniable Failure: The Progressive Movement." FreedomWorks. http://www.freedomworks.org/content/undeniable-failure-progressive-movement

Chapman, Michael W. "Bono: 'Capitalism Takes More People Out of Poverty Than Aid.'" CNS News. https://www.cnsnews.com/blog/michael-w-chapman/bono-capitalism-takes-more-people-out-poverty-aid

Clark, Josh. "Is a free market 'free' if it's regulated?" How Stuff Works. https://money.howstuffworks.com/free-market-economy2.htm

Davies, Stephen. "Top Three Myths about the Great Depression and the New Deal." Libertarianism. https://www.libertarianism.org/media/around-web/top-three-myths-about-great-depression-new-deal

Folsom, Burton W. "Myths of the New Deal." Foundation for Economic Education. https://fee.org/articles/myths-of-the-new-deal/

Forbes, Steve. "Capitalism: A True Love Story." *Forbes.*
https://www.forbes.com/forbes/2009/1019/opinions-steve-forbes-capitalism-true-love-story.html#434541a662de

Fulton, Joshua. "Welfare before the Welfare State." Mises Institute.
https://mises.org/library/welfare-welfare-state
(also referenced in a previous chapter)

Gordon, David. "The American Economy is Not a Free-Market Economy." Mises Institute.
https://mises.org/library/american-economy-not-free-market-economy

Harsanyi, David. "Liberals Were Very Wrong About Tax Cuts. Again." *Reason.*
https://reason.com/2019/05/10/liberals-were-very-wrong-about-tax-cuts-again/
(also referenced in a previous chapter)

Higgs, Robert. "The Mythology of Roosevelt and the New Deal." Independent Institute.
http://www.independent.org/publications/article.asp?id=176

McElwee, Charles F. "How Private Dollars Can Manage Public Parks." Manhattan Institute.
https://www.manhattan-institute.org/privatizing-parks-can-increase-real-estate-value

Moore, Stephen. "The Enduring Myth of FDR and the New Deal." The Heritage Foundation.

https://www.heritage.org/budget-and-spending/commentary/
the-enduring-myth-fdr-and-the-new-deal

Reed, Lawrence W. "Great Myths of the Great Depression."
Foundation for Economic Education.
https://fee.org/resources/great-myths-of-the-great-depression/

Rothbard, Murray. *The Progressive Era*. Mises Institute.
https://mises-media.s3.amazonaws.com/The%20
Progressive%20Era_0.pdf
(also referenced in a previous chapter)

Samuel, Peter. "Roads Without the State." Foundation for
Economic Education.
https://fee.org/articles/roads-without-the-state/

Scandlen, Greg. "Mutual Aid Societies: It's Amazing What
People Can Do Together." The Federalist.
http://thefederalist.com/2014/08/27/
mutual-aid-societies-its-amazing-what-people-can-do-together/
(also referenced in a previous chapter)

Tanner, Michael. "Capitalism's Triumph." *National Review*.
https://www.nationalreview.com/2013/09/
capitalisms-triumph-michael-tanner/

Weinberger, David. "The Myth That Standard Oil Was a
'Predatory Monopoly.'" Foundation for Economic Education.
https://fee.org/articles/
the-myth-that-standard-oil-was-a-predatory-monopoly/
(also referenced in a previous chapter)

Welch, Matt and Alexis Garcia. "When Democrats Loved Deregulation." Real Clear Policy. https://www.realclearpolicy.com/2018/12/13/when_democrats_loved_deregulation_40328.html

Woods, Thomas E. "No, the Free Market Did Not Cause the Financial Crisis." Daily Reckoning. https://dailyreckoning.com/ no-the-free-market-did-not-cause-the-financial-crisis/

Dumb Reason #31: They Believe Socialism is the Answer

Alger, Vicki E. "It's Time to Admit the Feds Are Making Poverty Worse--Not Better." The Daily Caller. https://www.iwf.org/2019/01/29/its-time-to-admit-the-feds-are-making-poverty-worse-not-better/ (also referenced in a previous chapter)

Bourne, Ryan. "No, Economists Don't Agree a 70 Percent Top Marginal Tax Rate Is a Good Idea." *Reason.* https://reason.com/archives/2019/01/09/ do-economists-agree-a-70-percent-top-mar

Cannon, Michael F. "Market Concentration in Health Care: Government Is the Problem, Not the Solution." Cato Institute. https://www.cato.org/briefing-paper/market-concentration-health-care-government-problem-not-solution

Chamberlin, William Henry. "European Socialism in Eclipse." Foundation for Economic Education. https://fee.org/articles/european-socialism-in-eclipse/

Da Silva, Giovanna. "Why the U.S. Should Adopt the Nordic Approach to Private Roads." The Devoe L. Moore Center Blog. https://devoelmoorecenter.com/2018/02/28/ why-the-u-s-should-adopt-the-nordic-approach-to-private-roads/

Davies, Antony and James R. Harrigan. "Transferism, Not Socialism, Is the Drug Americans Are Hooked On." Foundation for Economic Education. https://fee.org/articles/ transferism-not-socialism-is-the-drug-americans-are-hooked-on/

Editors. "Patients in most deprived areas wait 20 per cent longer for common heart procedure." University of York. https://www.york.ac.uk/news-and-events/news/2018/research/ patients-waiting-coronary/

Editors. "Thousands in Britain left to go blind due to eye surgery rationing: Report." *The Straits Times.* https://www.straitstimes.com/world/europe/thousands-in-britain-left-to-go-blind-due-to-eye-surgery-rationing-report

Edwards, Chris. "Higher Incomes, Higher Tax Rates." Cato Institute. https://www.cato.org/blog/higher-incomes-higher-tax-rates

Elder, Larry. "AOC returns to the scene of the minimum wage crime." Amac. https://www.amac.us/ aoc-returns-to-the-scene-of-the-minimum-wage-crime/

Firey, Thomas A. and Peter Van Doren. "Coronavirus and Regulation." Cato Institute.

https://www.cato.org/blog/coronavirus-regulation

Gillespie, Nick. "Increasing Top Tax Brackets Is Easier Than Increasing Revenue Over Time." *Reason.*
https://reason.com/blog/2019/01/06/
increasing-top-tax-brackets-is-easier-th

Gillespie, Nick and John Osterhoudt. "The FDA and CDC's Coronavirus Response Is a 'Failure of Historic Proportions.'" *Reason.*
https://reason.com/video/the-fda-and-cdcs-coronavirus-response-is-a-failure-of-historic-proportions/

Goldman, Samuel. "The Problem With Free College." The American Conservative.
https://www.theamericanconservative.com/articles/
the-problem-with-free-college/

Greenhut, Steven. "California's Rent Control Advocates Are About To Get What They Want, Good and Hard." *Reason.*
https://reason.com/2019/05/10/californias-rent-control-advocates-are-about-to-get-what-they-want-good-and-hard/

Hays, Charlotte. "Bipartisan Proposals on Drug Price Controls Threaten Innovation." Independent Women's Forum.
http://iwf.org/blog/2808372/Bipartisan-Proposals-on-Drug-Price-Controls-Threaten-Innovation

Heath, Allister. "France's failed socialist experiment is turning into a tragedy." City AM.
https://www.cityam.com/
france-s-failed-socialist-experiment-turning-tragedy/

Heath, Hadley. "How the Warren-Cortez 'Wealth Taxes' Would Undermine the Booming Economy." The Daily Caller. https://www.iwf.org/2019/02/05/how-the-warren-cortez-wealth-taxes-would-undermine-the-booming-economy/

Herzlinger, Regina E. and Bacchus Barua. "Europe's Alternative to Medicare for All." *Wall Street Journal.* https://www.wsj.com/articles/ europes-alternative-to-medicare-for-all-11555457596 (also referenced in a previous chapter)

Hoffower, Hillary. "College is more expensive than it's ever been, and the 5 reasons why suggest it's only going to get worse." *Business Insider.* https://www.businessinsider.com/ why-is-college-so-expensive-2018-4

Iacono, Corey. "The Myth of Scandinavian Socialism." Foundation for Economic Education. https://fee.org/articles/the-myth-of-scandinavian-socialism/

Kelly, Andrew P. "The Problem Is That Free College Isn't Free." *The New York Times.* https://www.nytimes.com/roomfordebate/2016/01/20/ should-college-be-free/the-problem-is-that-free-college-isnt-free

Koleilat Khatib, Dania. "France and the failure of socialism." UPI. https://www.upi.com/Top_News/Voices/2018/12/12/ France-and-the-failure-of-socialism/7591544527027/

Magness, Phillip W. "Even Swedish Socialism was Violent."
American Institute for Economic Research.
https://www.aier.org/article/even-swedish-socialism-was-violent
(also referenced in a previous chapter)

Magness, Phillip W. "The Big Fib about the Rich and Taxes."
American Institute for Economic Research.
https://aier.org/article/the-big-fib-about-the-rich-and-taxes/

Matzko, Paul. "To help solve the surgical mask shortage, get
the FDA out of the way." *New York Daily News.*
https://www.nydailynews.com/opinion/ny-oped-surgical-
masks-fda-20200401-vlwe72h76bb53hibyf5ddu6mou-story.
html

Miller, Henry I. and John J. Cohrssen. "A Market-Based
Solution to Rising Drug Prices: More Competition." American
Greatness.
https://amgreatness.com/2019/01/14/a-market-based-solution-
to-rising-drug-prices-more-competition/

Moffit, Robert. "Medicare's Financial Condition Is Getting
Worse. Here's What Trump and Congress Can Do." The Daily
Signal.
https://www.dailysignal.com/2019/02/20/medicares-financial-
condition-is-getting-worse-heres-what-trump-and-congress-
can-do/

Nolan Brown, Elizabeth. "Over-the-Counter Contraception Is
Immensely Popular. But Democrats Have Doomed It." *Reason.*
https://reason.com/archives/2019/01/16/deregulate-the-pill

Novak, Jake. "Why are we ignoring this colossal socialist failure?" *CNBC.*
https://www.cnbc.com/2015/07/01/greek-disaster-is-all-about-socialism.html

Riedl, Brian. "Money to Burn." Manhattan Institute.
https://www.manhattan-institute.org/money-to-burn-2020-presidential-race-democrats

Riedl, Brian. "Why 70 Percent Tax Rates Cannot Finance Socialism." Manhattan Institute.
https://www.manhattan-institute.org/html/ocasio-cortez-70-percent-tax-socialism

Sabino, Carlos. "From Venezuela to France, Socialism Is Failing All Over the World." *PanAm Post.*
https://en.panampost.com/carlos-sabino/2017/04/27/socialism-is-failing-all-over-the-world/

Sandler, Rachel. "How the CDC Botched Its Initial Coronavirus Response With Faulty Tests." *Forbes.*
https://www.forbes.com/sites/rachelsandler/2020/03/02/how-the-cdc-botched-its-initial-coronavirus-response-with-faulty-tests/#e702f10670ef

Stainburn, Samantha. "Catching Up on the Bennett Hypothesis." *The New York Times.*
https://www.nytimes.com/2013/11/03/education/edlife/catching-up-on-the-bennett-hypothesis.html

Stephens, Bret. "Yes, Venezuela Is a Socialist Catastrophe." *New York Times.*

https://www.nytimes.com/2019/01/25/opinion/venezuela-maduro-socialism-government.html

Stossel, John and Tanvir Toy. "Sweden Is Not a Socialist Success." *Reason.*
https://reason.com/reasontv/2018/10/23/stossel-sweden-not-a-socialist-success

Stossel, John and Tanvir Toy. "The Paid Leave Fairy Tale." *Reason.*
https://reason.com/video/stossel-the-paid-leave-fairy-tale/

Wolfram, Gary. "Making College More Expensive: The Unintended Consequences of Federal Tuition Aid." Cato Institute.
https://www.cato.org/publications/policy-analysis/making-college-more-expensive-unintended-consequences-federal-tuition-aid

Dumb Reason #32: They Are "Pro-Union" and "Pro-Labor"

Levitz, Eric. "Democrats Paid a Huge Price for Letting Unions Die." *New York Magazine.*
http://nymag.com/intelligencer/2018/01/democrats-paid-a-huge-price-for-letting-unions-die.html

Seitz-Wald, Alex. "Democrats love unions. Just not for their own campaign workers." *NBC News.*
https://www.nbcnews.com/politics/elections/democrats-love-unions-just-not-their-own-campaign-workers-n864196

Stossel, John. "Public-Sector Unions Choke Taxpayers."
Creators Syndicate.
https://www.creators.com/read/john-stossel/10/10/
public-sector-unions-choke-taxpayers--c7198

Stossel, John. "Why unions are bad for workers."
WorldNetDaily.
https://www.wnd.com/2012/05/
why-unions-are-bad-for-workers/

Dumb Reason #33: They Are Elitist When It Comes to
Geography

Azzerad, Davis. "America Divided: It Starts With the
Democratic Party." The Heritage Foundation.
https://www.heritage.org/progressivism/commentary/
america-divided-it-starts-the-democratic-party

Radke, Amanda. "Mainstream media slams flyover states as
rural voters unite to elect Trump." *Beef Magazine.*
https://www.beefmagazine.com/blog/mainstream-media-slams-
flyover-states-rural-voters-unite-elect-trump

Dumb Reason #34: They Believe the Best Presidents Are the
Ones that Do the Most

Buchanan, Patrick J. "Ranking the Presidents." *The American
Conservative.*
https://www.theamericanconservative.com/articles/
ranking-the-presidents/

Healy, Gene. "Activist and Warrior Presidents Dominate Historians' Polls." Cato Institute. https://www.cato.org/publications/commentary/activist-warrior-presidents-dominate-historians-polls

Kengor, Paul. "Rating the Presidents — and Obama." *The American Spectator.* https://spectator.org/rating-the-presidents-and-obama/

McDonald, Matt. "Political Science Hacks Create Totally Fair and Unbiased Ranking of U.S. Presidents." *New Boston Post.* https://newbostonpost.com/2018/02/21/political-science-hacks-create-totally-fair-and-unbiased-ranking-of-u-s-presidents/

Dumb Reason #35: They Believe Life is Unfair Due to "Privilege"

Duke, Selwyn. "The Myth of White Privilege." American Thinker. https://www.americanthinker.com/articles/2011/07/the_myth_of_white_privilege.html

Prager, Dennis. "The Fallacy of 'White Privilege.'" *National Review.* https://www.nationalreview.com/2016/02/white-privilege-myth-reality/ (also also referenced in a previous chapter)

Dumb Reason #36: They Are Against War

Editors. "Don't Let Democrats Become the Party of War." Veterans Today.

https://www.veteranstoday.com/2019/02/04/
dont-let-democrats-become-the-party-of-war/

Harrigan, Fiona. "America's Involvement in Ukraine
Increasingly Looks Like War." *Reason*.
https://reason.com/2022/07/01/
americas-involvement-in-ukraine-increasingly-looks-like-war/

Hochman, Nate. "Democrats Care More Democrats Care
More about Ukraine's Border Than Ours about Ukraine's
Border Than Ours." *National Review*.
https://www.nationalreview.com/corner/
democrats-care-more-about-ukraines-border-than-ours/

Osterweil, Willie. "Democrats Are the Real Party of War." The
Baffler.
https://thebaffler.com/latest/democrats-are-the-real-party-of-war

Turse, Nick. "How Many Wars Is the US Really Fighting?" The
Nation.
https://www.thenation.com/article/archive/
how-many-wars-is-the-us-really-fighting/

Dumb Reason #37: They Support Immigration

Albright, Logan. "Can We Stop Pretending Democrats Care
About Black People, Immigrants?" FreedomWorks.
http://www.freedomworks.org/content/can-we-stop-pretending-
democrats-care-about-black-people-immigrants
(also referenced in a previous chapter)

Beinart, Peter. "How the Democrats Lost Their Way on Immigration." RealClear Politics. https://www.realclearpolitics.com/2017/06/20/how_the_democrats_lost_their_way_on_immigration_413523.html

Editors. "NYC, DC mayors complain about illegal immigrants bused from TX, AZ." American Military News. https://americanmilitarynews.com/2022/07/nyc-dc-mayors-complain-about-illegal-immigrants-bused-from-tx-az/

Enten, Harry. "Democrats Weren't Always Super Liberal On Immigration." FiveThirtyEight. https://fivethirtyeight.com/features/democrats-werent-always-super-liberal-on-immigration/

Mikelionis, Lukas. "Democrats' illegal immigration tune has changed over years despite incoming caravan." *Fox News.* https://www.foxnews.com/politics/democrats-illegal-immigration-tune-has-changed-over-years-despite-incoming-caravan

Williams, Walter E. "Politics of Immigration." Townhall. https://townhall.com/columnists/walterewilliams/2019/01/16/politics-of-immigration-n2538997

Dumb Reason #38: They Are Anti-Israel

Diker, Dan. "Israel's Settlements: Legal or Illegal?" Jerusalem Center for Public Affairs. https://youtu.be/om8PS8R0s9Q

Elder, Larry. "The truth about Israel's 'stolen' land."
WorldNetDaily.
https://www.wnd.com/2009/01/85547/

Elder, Larry. "Why There Can Never Be 'Peace in the Middle
East.'" Townhall.
https://townhall.com/columnists/larryelder/2014/07/24/
why-there-can-never-be-peace-in-the-middle-east-n1865224

Friedman, Matti. "There Is No 'Israeli-Palestinian Conflict.'"
The New York Times.
https://www.nytimes.com/2019/01/16/opinion/israeli-
palestinian-conflict-matti-friedman.html

Horowitz, David. "Why Israel Is the Victim." *Frontpage
Magazine.*
https://www.frontpagemag.com/fpm/177041/
why-israel-victim-david-horowitz

Prager, Dennis. "The Middle East Problem." PragerU.
https://www.prageru.com/video/the-middle-east-problem/

Richman, Rick. "It's Not the Settlements, Stupid." *Commentary
Magazine.*
https://www.commentary.org/rick-richman/
its-not-the-settlements-stupid/

Williams, Armstrong. "In Defense of Israel." Townhall.
https://townhall.com/columnists/
armstrongwilliams/2018/07/26/in-defense-of-israel-n2503701

Dumb Reason #39: They Think Being Liberals Means Being Kind and Caring

Mace, Maryann. "Democrats care more about people than the GOP." *St. Louis Post – Dispatch.* https://www.stltoday.com/opinion/mailbag/democrats-care-more-about-people-than-the-gop/article_6d068738-00d0-5810-9820-0e8dffc35e66.html

McDonald, Joel. "Democrats Care About People." LGBT Democrats of Virginia. https://lgbtvadem.org/2014/03/democrats-care-about-people/